Acoustic Rock

ISBN 978-0-634-05061-9

HAL•LEONARD® CORPORATION

7777 W. BLUEMOUND RD. P.O. BOX 13819 MILWAUKEE, WI 53213

Visit Hal Leonard Online at
www.halleonard.com

Guitar Chord Songbook

Contents

Angie

Words and Music by Mick Jagger
and Keith Richards

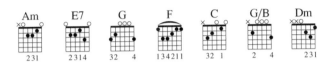

Verse 1

　　　　Am　　　**E7**
　　　Angie,　　Angie,

G　　　　　　　**F**　　　　　　　　**C**　　**G/B**
　　When will those clouds all disappear?

Am　　　**E7**
　　Angie, Angie,

G　　　　　**F**　　　　**C**
　　Where will it lead us from here?

　　　　　　G
With no loving in our souls

　　　　Dm　　　　　　　　**Am**
And no money in our coats,

C　　　　　　**F**　　　　　　　**G**
　　You can't say___ we're satisfied.

　　　Am　　**E7**
But Angie, Angie,

G　　　　　**F**　　　　　　**C**
　　You can't say we never tried.

Verse 2

```
            Am                      E7
            A - Angie, you're beautiful,

            G            F                    C       G/B
            But ain't it time we said goodbye?

            Am           E7
            A - Angie,    I still love ya.

            G                   F              C
            Remember all__ those nights we cried?

            G
            All the dreams__ we held so close

                        Dm          Am
            Seemed to all__ go up in smoke.

            C                     F              G
            Uh, let me whis-per in your ear:

             Am    E7
            "Angie, Angie,

            G          F          C
            Where will it lead us from here?"
```

Bridge

```
                  G
            Oh, Angie, don't you weep.

                        Dm          Am
            All your kiss - es still taste sweet.

            C              F                G
            I hate that sadness in your eyes.

                  Am    E7
            But Angie, Angie,

            G              F              C
            Ain't it time__ we said good-bye?
```

Outro

       G
With no loving in our souls

       Dm   **Am**
And no money in our coats,

C   **F**   **G**
You can't say__ we're satisfied.

       Dm   **Am**
But Angie, I still love you, ba - by.

Dm   **Am**
Ev'rywhere I look I see your eyes.

Dm   **Am**
There ain't a woman that comes close to you.

C   **F**   **G**
Come on, ba - by, dry your eyes.

       Am   **E7**
But Angie, Angie,

G   **F**   **C**   **G/B**
Ain't it good to be alive?

Am   **E7**
Angie, Angie,

G   **F**   **C**
They can't say we never tried.

About a Girl

Words and Music by Kurt Cobain

Tune down 1/2 step:
(low to high) Eb–Ab–Db–Gb–Bb–Eb

Melody:

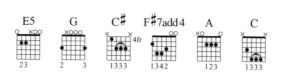

I need an eas-y friend, ___

E5   G   C#   F#7add4   A   C

Intro   ‖: E5   G | E5   G   :‖   *Play 4 times*

Verse 1

E5 G   E5   G
I   need an easy friend,

E5 G   E5   G
I do,   with an ear to lend.

E5 G   E5   G
I do   think you fit this shoe,

E5 G   E5   G
I do,   but you have a clue.

Chorus 1

C#   F#7add4
I'll take ad-vantage while

C#   F#7add4
You hang me out to dry,

E5   A C
But I can't see you ev'ry night

E5 G   E5 G
For free.

E5 G   E5 G
I do.

Verse 2

E5 G   E5   G
I'm standing in your line,

E5 G   E5   G
I do, hope you have the time.

E5 G   E5   G
I do, pick a number to,

E5 G   E5   G
I do, keep a date with you.

Chorus 2

Repeat Chorus 1

Guitar Solo

Repeat Verse 1 (Instrumental)
Repeat Chorus 1 (Instrumental)

Verse 3

Repeat Verse 1

Chorus 3

C♯   F♯7add4
  I'll take ad-vantage while

C♯   F♯7add4
  You hang me out to dry,

  E5   A C
But I can't see you ev'ry night.

E5   A C
I can't see you ev'ry night

  E5 G E5   G
For free.

E5   G E5   G
I do.

E5   G E5   G
I do.

E5   G E5   G
I do.

E5
I do.

Across the Universe

Melody:

Words and Music by
John Lennon and Paul McCartney

Words are flow-ing out __ like end - less...

D   F#m   F#sus4   A   Aadd9   Dmaj7

F#m*   Em7   A7   A7*   Gm   G

Intro

| D | | F#m F#sus4 F#m F#sus4 F#m F#sus4 F#m F#sus4 |

| A Aadd9 A Aadd9 A Aadd9 A Aadd9 |

Verse 1

D   Dmaj7   F#m*
Words are flowing out__ like endless rain into a paper cup,

Em7   A7   A7*
They slither while they pass they slip away__ across the universe.

D   Dmaj7   F#m*
Pools of sorrow, waves of joy are drifting through my open mind,

Em7   Gm
Pos-sessing and ca-ressing me.

Chorus 1

D   A7
Jai. Guru. Deva. Om.

Nothing's gonna change my world,

G   D
Nothing's gonna change my world.

A7
Nothing's gonna change my world,

G   D
Nothing's gonna change my world.

| | D   Dmaj7   F♯m*   Em7 |
| *Verse 2* | Images of broken light which dance before me like a million eyes, |

A7   A7*
They call me on and on across__ the universe.

D   Dmaj7   F♯m*
Thoughts meander like a restless wind inside a letter box,

Em7   A7
They tumble blindly as they make their way across the universe.

Chorus 2   *Repeat Chorus 1*

| | D   Dmaj7   F♯m* |
| *Verse 3* | Sounds of laughter, shades of life are ringing through my open ears, |

Em7   Gm
In-citing and in-viting me.

D   Dmaj7   F#m*   Em7
Limitless, un-dying love which shines around me like a million suns,

A7   A7*
It calls me on and on a-cross the universe.

Chorus 3   *Repeat Chorus 1*

| | D |
| *Outro* | ‖: Jai. Guru. Deva. :‖ *Play 6 times and fade* |

Back to You

Words and Music by
Bryan Adams and Eliot Kennedy

Melody:

I've been down, __ I've been beat, __

C   Am   F   Gsus4   G   E7   Em   Dm

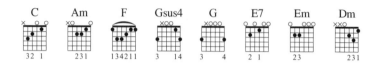

Intro ‖: C   Am | F | Gsus4 | G   :‖

Verse 1

```
            C              Am
I've been down, ___ I've been beat,
       F              Gsus4
I've been so tired I could not speak.
   G    C                    Am
I've been so lost ___ that I could not see
       F                    Gsus4
I wanted things that were out of reach.
G    C                        Am
Then I ___ found you and you helped me through.
       F                    Gsus4
Yeah, you showed me what to do.
   G        F                    E7
And that's why ___ I'm comin' back to you, yeah.
```

GUITAR CHORD SONGBOOK

	Am F Gsus4 G
Chorus 1	Like a star ___ guides a ship across the o - cean

Am   F   Gsus4   G
Is how your love ___ can take me home, back to you.

                        Em   Am
And if I wish ___ upon that star,

                        Em   Am
Someday I'll be where you are.

                        Dm   Gsus4
And I know that day is coming soon.

                        G   C
Yeah, I'm com - in' back to you.

Interlude	| C Am | F | Gsus4|

	G C Am
Verse 2	You've been alone, ___ but you did not show it.

                        F   Gsus4
You've been in pain when I did not know it.

                        G   C   Am
You let me do ___ what I needed to.

                        F   Gsus4
You were there when I needed you.

G   C   Am
Might a let ___ you down, might a messed you around,

                        F   Gsus4
But you never changed your point of view.

                        G   F   E7
And that's why ___ I'm comin' back to you, yeah.

Chorus 2	*Repeat Chorus 1*
Dobro Solo	*Repeat Intro*

Verse 3

    G   C   Am
Might a let ____ you down, might a messed you around,

        F   Gsus4
But you never changed your point of view.

     G   F   E7
And that's why ____ I'm comin' back to you, yeah.

Chorus 3

                Am   F   Gsus4 G
Like a star ____ guides a ship across the o - cean

                   Am   F   Gsus4 G
Is how your love ____ can take me home, back to you.

        Em   Am
And if I wish ____ upon that star,

        Em   Am
Someday I'll be where you are.

       Dm   Gsus4
And I know that day is coming soon.

     G   Am
Oh,   I'm comin' back to you.

Outro

‖: Am   F | |
| Gsus4 | G   :‖ *Play 3 times*
                  I'm comin' back to you.

| Am   F | |
| Gsus4 | G |
                  That day is comin' soon.

| Am   F | |
| Gsus4 | G |
                  I'm comin' back to you.

| Am   F | |
| Gsus4 | G |
          Yeah.

| Am | F |C

Behind Blue Eyes

Words and Music by Pete Townshend

Melody:

No one knows _ what it's like _ to be the bad man, _

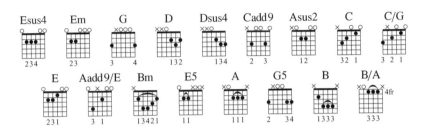

Intro

| Esus4 | | |

Verse 1

   Em   **G**
No one knows what it's like

      D   **Dsus4 D**
To be the bad man,

           Cadd9   **Asus2**
To be the sad man behind ____ blue eyes.

Em   **G**
No one knows what it's like

      D   **Dsus4 D**
To be hated,

        Cadd9   **Asus2**
To be fated to telling on - ly lies.

Chorus 1

        C   D   G   C/G G
But my dreams, ____ they aren't as empty

        C   D   E Aadd9/E E
As my conscience seems to be.

        Bm   C
I have hours only lone - ly.

                D   Dsus4
My love is ven - geance

D   Asus2
That's never free.

Verse 2

Em   G
No one knows what it's like

            D
To feel these feelings

        Cadd9   Asus2
Like I do, ____ and I blame you.

Em   G
No one bites back as hard

        D
On their anger,

        Cadd9   Asus2
None of my pain and woe can show through.

Chorus 2   *Repeat Chorus 1*

Interlude 1 |E5   Bm| A E5| Bm| A E5|

Verse 3

        E5   Bm   A   E5
When my fist clenches, crack it open

     Bm   G5   D
Before I use it and lose my cool.

     Bm A   D
When I smile, tell me some bad news

     Bm A   E5   Bm A E5
Before I laugh and act like a fool.

     Bm   A   E5
And if I swallow anything evil,

     Bm   G5   D
Put your finger down my ____ throat.

     Bm   A   D
And if I shiver, please ____ give me a blanket,

     Bm   A   E5
Keep me warm, let me wear your coat.

Interlude 2

E5	Bm		A	E5		Bm		A	B
A	G5	D	B			A	G5	D	B
A	G5	D	B			B/A			

Outro

     Em   G
No one knows what it's like

     D   Dsus4 D
To be the bad man,

     Cadd9   Asus2
To be the sad man behind ____ blue eyes.

Band on the Run

Words and Music by McCartney

Melody:

Stuck in - side these four   walls, _____

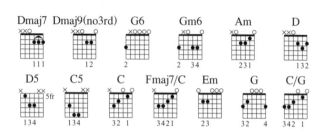

Dmaj7	Dmaj9(no3rd)	G6	Gm6	Am	D
D5	C5	C	Fmaj7/C	Em	G	C/G

Intro   ‖: Dmaj7 | Dmaj9(no3rd) | G6 | :‖
            | Dmaj7 | Gm6 | Dmaj7 | Gm6 |

Dmaj7   **Dmaj9(no3rd)**

Verse 1   Stuck inside these four walls,

G6
Sent inside forever.

Dmaj7   **Dmaj9(no3rd)**
Never seeing no one

G6   **Dmaj7**
Nice again like you,

Gm6 Dmaj7 Gm6 Dmaj7 Gm6
Mama, you,   Mama, you.

Interlude 1   ‖: Am | D | Am | D | Am :‖

Verse 2

Am
If I ever get out of here,

D
Thought of giving it all away

Am
To a registered charity.

D
All I need is a pint a day.

Am
If I ever get out of here. (If we ever get out of here.)

Interlude 2

| N.C.   ‖:D5   C5 | N.C.   :‖

| C | Fmaj7/C | C | Fmaj7/C

Verse 3

C   Fmaj7/C
Well, the rain exploded with a mighty crash

C
As we fell into the sun.

Fmaj7/C
And the first one said to the second one there

Em
I hope you're having fun.

Chorus 1

G   C
Band on the run,

Em C   Am
Band on the run.

      Fmaj7/C   C
And the jailer man and sailor Sam

    Fmaj7/C
Were searching ev'ryone.

      C   Fmaj7/C C Fmaj7/C
For the band on the run,

C   Fmaj7   C   Fmaj7/C
Band on the run.

      C   Fmaj7/C C Fmaj7/C
For the band on the run,

C   Fmaj7/C C Fmaj7/C
Band on the run.

Verse 4

        C   Fmaj7/C
Well, the undertaker drew a heavy sigh

               C
Seeing no one else had come.

           Fmaj7/C
And a bell was ringing in the village square

          Em
For the rabbits on the run.

Chorus 2

G   C
Band on the run,

Em C   Am
Band on the run.

      Fmaj7/C   C
And the jailer man and sailor Sam

    Fmaj7/C
Were searching ev'ryone.

      C   Fmaj7/C C Fmaj7/C
For the band on the run,

C   Fmaj7/C C Fmaj7/C
Band on the run.

Interlude 3

```
| Em   G   C/G  | Em   C   Am   |Fmaj7/C           |
| C             | Fmaj7/C        |                  |
```

Chorus 3

       C   Fmaj7/C C Fmaj7/C
Yeah, the band on the run,

    C   Fmaj7/C C Fmaj7/C
The band on the run.

    C   Fmaj7/C C Fmaj7/C
The band on the run,

C   Fmaj7/C C Fmaj7/C
Band on the run.

Verse 5

      C   Fmaj7/C
Well, the night was falling as the desert world

            C
Began to settle down.

                  Fmaj7/C
In the town they're searching for us ev'rywhere

            Em
But we never will be found.

Chorus 4

G   C
Band on the run,

Em C   Am
Band on the run.

    Fmaj7/C   C
And the county judge held a grudge;

    Fmaj7/C
Will search forevermore

      C   Fmaj7/C C Fmaj7/C
For the band on the run,

    C   Fmaj7/C C Fmaj7/C
The band on the run.

    C   Fmaj7/C C Fmaj7/C
The band on the run,

    C   Fmaj7/C C Fmaj7/C Em G C
The band on the run.

Best of My Love

Words and Music by John David Souther,
Don Henley and Glenn Frey

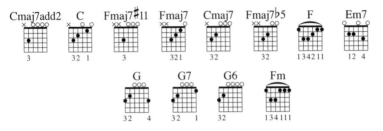

Intro

‖: Cmaj7add2 C |Cmaj7add2 C |
| Fmaj7#11 Fmaj7 |Fmaj7#11 Fmaj7 :‖

Verse 1

Cmaj7 C
Ev - ery night

Cmaj7 C
I'm ly - in' in bed

Fmaj7b5 Fmaj7   **Fmaj7b5 Fmaj7**
Hold - in' you close in my dreams;

Cmaj7 C
Think - in' about all the things that we said

   F
And comin' apart at the seams.

Em7   **Dm7**
We tried to talk it o - ver

    Em7   **F**
But the words come out too rough.

  Cmaj7 C
I know you were tryin'

   Fmaj7   **Cmaj7 C**   **G G7 G6 G7**
To give me the best of your love.

Verse 2

Cmaj7 C
Beau - tiful faces,

    Cmaj7 C
An' loud   empty places.

Fmaj7b5 Fmaj7   **Fmaj7b5 Fmaj7**
   Look at the way that we live,

Cmaj7 C
Wast - in' our time

On cheap talk and wine

F
   Left us so little to give.

Em7
   The same old crowd

    Dm7
Was like a cold dark cloud

        Em7   **F**
That we could never rise above,

    Cmaj7 C
But here   in my heart

    Fmaj7   **G**
I give you the best of my love.

Chorus 1

      C
Whoa,___ sweet darlin',

           F
You get the best of my love,

(You get the best of my love.)

    Cmaj7
Whoa,___ sweet darlin',

              F
You get the best of my love.

(You get the best of my love.)

Bridge

      Fm
Oo, I'm goin' back in time

      Cmaj7
And it's a sweet dream.

      Fm
It was a quiet night

And I would be alright

      Dm7   G7
If I could go on sleeping.

Verse 3

      Cmaj7 C
But ev - ery morning

     Cmaj7 C
I wake up and worry

Fmaj7b5 F
      What's gonna happen today.

Cmaj7 C
You   see it your way,

     Cmaj7 C
And I   see it mine,

      F
But we both see it slippin' away.

Em7   **Dm7**
    You know, we always had each other, baby.

     Em7   **F**
I guess that wasn't e-nough.

      Cmaj7 C
Oh, but here   in my heart

    Fmaj7   **Cmaj7 C**   **G**
I give you the best of my love.

Chorus 2   *Repeat Chorus 1 till fade*

Bridge Over Troubled Water

Words and Music by Paul Simon

When you're   wea - ry, ___

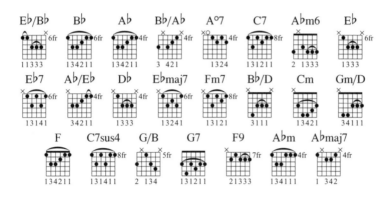

Intro

Eb/Bb	Bb	Ab	Bb/Ab A°7	Eb/Bb	C7	
Ab	Abm6	Eb	Eb7	Ab/Eb	
Eb	Eb7	Ab Eb	

Verse 1

            Eb   Ab/Eb   Eb
When you're weary,   feelin'___ small,

Ab   Db   Ab Ebmaj7   Fm7
   When tears are in your eyes,

Eb   Ab   Eb   Ab
I'll dry them all.

Eb Bb/D Cm   Bb
I'm on   your side.

               Eb   Gm/D
Oh, when times get rough,

Eb7   Ab   F   Bb
   And friends just can't be found,

Chorus 1

E♭   B♭ A♭   B♭/A♭ A°7 E♭/B♭   C7sus4 C7
Like a bridge o - ver troubled water,

A♭   G/B   Cm
  I will lay me down.

E♭   B♭ A♭   B♭/A♭ A°7 E♭/B♭   C7sus4 C7
Like a bridge o - ver troubled water,

A♭   G/B   E♭   E♭7
  I will lay me down.

| A♭/E♭ | | E♭ E♭7 | A♭/E♭ | | E♭ | | A♭/E♭ | |

Verse 2

          E♭
When you're down and out,

A♭/E♭   E♭
  When you're on the ___ street,

A♭   D♭ A♭ E♭maj7   Fm7
  When eve-ning falls so hard

     E♭   A♭   E♭   A♭
I will comfort you.

E♭ B♭/D Cm   B♭
  I'll take your part.

              E♭   Gm/D
Oh, when darkness comes,

E♭7   A♭ F   B♭
  And pain is all around,

Chorus 2

E♭   B♭ A♭   B♭/A♭ A°7 E♭/B♭   C7sus4 C7
Like a bridge o - ver troubled water,

A♭   G/B   Cm
  I will lay me down.

E♭   B♭ A♭   B♭/A♭ A°7 E♭/B♭   Cm
Like a bridge o - ver troubled water,

A♭   G7   Cm   F9
  I will lay me down.

Interlude

Eb/Bb Bb	Ab Cm	Ab Abm	Eb	
Ab/Eb	Eb Eb7	Ab/Eb	Eb	
Ab/Eb				

Verse 3

Eb Ab/Eb Eb
Sail on silver girl, sail on ___ by.

Ab Db Ab Eb   Fm7
Your time has come to shine.

Eb   Ab   Eb   Ab
All your dreams are on their way.

Eb Bb/D Cm Bb
See how   they shine.

Eb Gm/D
Oh, if you need a friend

Eb7   Ab F Bb
I'm sailing right behind.

Chorus 3

Eb Bb Ab Bb/Ab A°7 Eb/Bb Cm
Like a bridge o - ver troubled water,

Ab G/B   Cm
I will ease your mind.

Eb7 Ab Abmaj7 Eb/Bb Cm
Like a bridge   over   troubled water,

Ab G7   Cm   F9
I will ease your mind.

| Eb/Bb Bb | Ab Cm | |
| Ab Abm | Eb | |

Blackbird

Words and Music by
John Lennon and Paul McCartney

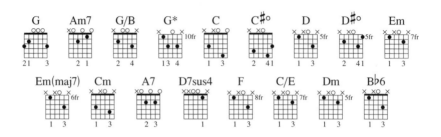

Intro

| G   Am7   G/B | G* |

Verse 1

G   Am7   G/B   G*
Blackbird singing in the dead of night,

C   C#°   D   D#°   Em   Em(maj7)
Take these broken wings__ and learn__ to fly.

D C#°   C   Cm
All your life,

G/B   A7   D7sus4   G
You were only wait - ing for this mo - ment to arise.

| C   G/B   A7 | D7sus4   G |

Verse 2

G   Am7   G/B   G*
Blackbird singing in the dead of night,

C   C#°   D   D#°   Em   Em(maj7)
Take these sunken eyes__ and learn__ to see.

D C#°   C   Cm
All your life,

G/B   A7   D7sus4   G
You were only wait - ing for this mo - ment to be free.

Bridge 1

F   C/E   Dm C   B♭6   C
Black - bird,___ fly.

F   C/E   Dm C   B♭6   A7
Black - bird,___ fly.

         D7sus4   **G**
Into the light_____ of a dark black night.

Interlude 1

|G Am7 G/B |G* |C C♯° D D♯° |Em Em(maj7) |

|D   C♯° |C Cm |G/B A7 |D7sus4 G |

Bridge 2

Repeat Bridge 1

Interlude 2

|G Am7 G/B |G* | | |

|G Am7 G/B C |G/B A7 D7sus4 |

Verse 3

G   Am7   G/B   G*
Blackbird singing in the dead of night,

C   C♯°   D   D♯°   Em Em(maj7)
Take these broken wings__ and learn__ to fly.

D C♯° C   Cm
All your life,

G/B   A7   D7sus4   G
You were only wait - ing for this mo - ment to arise.

C   G/B   A7   D7sus4   G
You were on - ly wait - ing for this mo - ment to arise.

C   G/B   A7   D7sus4   G
You were on - ly waiting__ for this mo - ment to arise.

Blowin' in the Wind

Words and Music by Bob Dylan

Melody:

How man-y roads

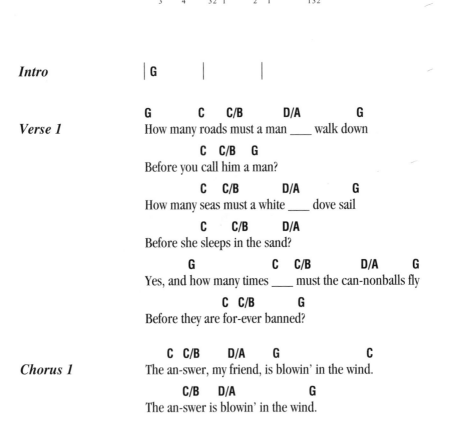

(Capo 7th fret)

G   C   C/B   D/A

Intro | G | | |

Verse 1

G   C   C/B   D/A   G
How many roads must a man ____ walk down
      C   C/B   G
Before you call him a man?
      C   C/B   D/A   G
How many seas must a white ____ dove sail
      C   C/B   D/A
Before she sleeps in the sand?
      G   C   C/B   D/A   G
Yes, and how many times ____ must the can-nonballs fly
      C   C/B   G
Before they are for-ever banned?

Chorus 1

      C   C/B   D/A   G   C
The an-swer, my friend, is blowin' in the wind.
      C/B   D/A   G
The an-swer is blowin' in the wind.

| Interlude 1 | `| C   C/B | D/A    | G      | C      |` |
| | `|     C/B | D/A    | G      |        |` |

Verse 2

```
                 G              C  C/B      D/A      G
Yes, and how many years__ can a moun - tain exist
          C      C/B    G
Before it is washed to the sea?
                 C    C/B      D/A      G
Yes, and how many years can some people exist
               C    C/B      D/A
Before they're al-lowed to be free?
                 G              C  C/B      D/A              G
Yes, and how many times ____ can a man ____ turn his head
                  C   C/B      G
And pretend that he just__ doesn't see?
```

Chorus 2　　　*Repeat Chorus 1*

Interlude 2　　*Repeat Interlude 1*

Verse 3

```
                 G      C    D/A          G
Yes, and how many   times must a man look up
                C   C/B      G
Before he can see _____ the sky?
                        C    D/A      G
Yes, and how many ears ____ must one man have
               C  C/B  D/A
Before he can hear __ people cry?
                 G      C    C/B  D/A          G
Yes, and how many deaths will it take till he knows
                  C          C/B  G
That too many peo - ple have died?
```

Chorus 3　　　*Repeat Chorus 1*

Outro　　　　*Repeat Interlude 1*

Blue Suede Shoes

Words and Music by Carl Lee Perkins

Melody:

Well, it's   one   for the mon - ey,...

A   D9   E9

                              A   N.C.   A

Verse 1   Well, it's one for the money,   two for the show,

              N.C.   **A**
Three to get ready, now go, cat, go,

              D9   **A**
But don't__ you step on my blue suede shoes.

              E9   **A**
Well, you can do anything but lay off of my blue suede shoes.

              A   **N.C.**   **A**   **N.C.**   **A**

Verse 2   Well, you can knock me down,   step on my face,

              N.C.   **A**   **N.C.**   **A**
Slander my name all over the place.

              N.C.   **A**   **N.C.** **A**
Well, do any - thing __ that you wanna do,

              N.C.   **A**
But uh-uh, honey, lay off__ of them shoes

              D9   **A**
And don't__ you step on my blue suede shoes.

              E9   **A**
Well, you can do anything but lay off of my blue suede shoes.

Let's go cats!

Solo 1

```
| A          |         |         |         |
| D9    |    | A    |    |         |
| E9    |    | A    |    |         |
```

Verse 3

                 A   N.C.   A   N.C.   A
Well, you can burn my house,   steal my car,

             N.C.   A   N.C.   A
Drink my li-quor from an old fruit jar.

                  N.C. A   N.C. A
Well, do any-thing that you wan-na do,

           N.C.   A
But uh-uh, honey, lay off__ of them shoes

               D9   A
And don't__ you step on my blue suede shoes.

                E9   A
Well, you can do anything but lay off of my blue suede shoes.

Rock it!

Solo 2   *Repeat Solo 1*

Verse 4   *Repeat Verse 1*

Outro

               A
Well, it's   blue, blue, blue suede shoes,

Blue, blue, blue suede shoes, yeah.

D9
    Blue, blue, blue suede shoes, baby.

A
    Blue, blue, blue suede shoes.

               E9   A
Well, you can do anything but lay off of my blue suede shoes.

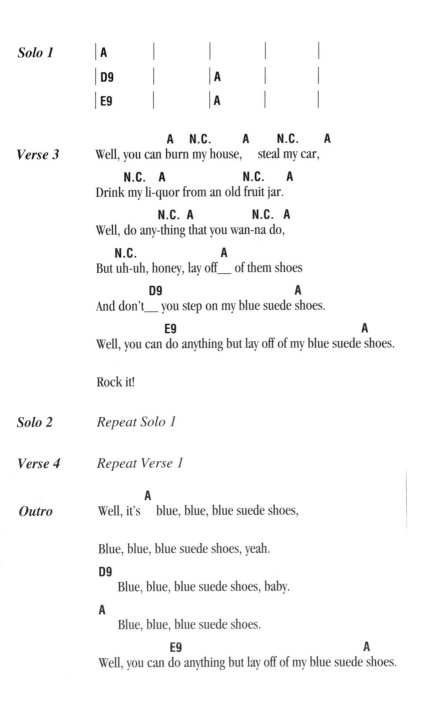

Catch the Wind

Words and Music by Donovan Leitch

Melody:

In the chil-ly _____ hours and

(Capo 3rd fret)

C   Fadd9   G   F   G7   Em   D/A   G6   G7*

Intro

| C | | | Fadd9 | G | |
| C | | Fadd9 | C | | |

Verse 1

        C   Fadd9   C
In the chilly hours and minutes of un-certainty

  F   C   Fadd9 G   C   G7
I want to be in the warm hold of your lovin' mind.

   C   Fadd9
To feel you all a-round me

   C   F
And to take your hand a-long the sand.

 C   Fadd9 G   C   Fadd9 C
Ah, but I may as well try and catch the wind.

Verse 2

        C   Fadd9
When sundown pales the sky,

        C   F
I want to hide awhile behind your smile,

C   Fadd9   G   C   G7
And ev'rywhere I'd look, your eyes I'd find.

      C   Fadd9
For me to love you now

          C   F
Would be the sweetest thing, 'twould make me sing.

C   Fadd9 G   C   Fadd9   C
Ah, but I may as well try and catch the wind.

Bridge

F   Em
De, de, de, de, de, de, de, de.

      F   D/A
De, de, de, de, de, de, de, de,

     G G6 G7* G6
De, de, de.

Verse 3

       C   Fadd9
When rain has hung the leaves with tears,

C   F
I want you near to kill my fears,

C   Fadd9 G   C   G7
To help me to leave all my blues be-hind.

      C   Fadd9
For standing in your heart

         C   F
Is where I want to be, and long to be.

C   Fadd9 G   C   Fadd9   C
Ah, but I may as well try and catch the wind.

Harp Solo   *Repeat Verse 1 (Instrumental)*

Outro

| C | | | Fadd9 | | |
| C | | | F | | |

      C   Fadd9 G   C   Fadd9   C
Ah, but I may as well try and catch the wind.

Change the World

Words and Music by Wayne Kirkpatrick,
Gordon Kennedy and Tommy Sims

Melody:

If I could reach the __ stars, __

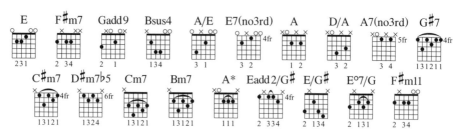

Intro

E F♯m7 Gadd9	
F♯m7 E	
F♯m7 Gadd9	
F♯m7 Bsus4	

Verse 1

    E   A/E   E7(no 3rd)
If I could reach the __ stars,

        A/E   E
Pull one down for you.

      A/E   E7(no 3rd)
Shine it on my heart

        A/E   E
So you could see the truth.

   A   D/A   A7(no 3rd)
That this love I have in - side

      D/A   A
Is ev'ry-thing it seems.

   E   A/E   E7(no 3rd)
But for now I find

      A/E   G♯7
It's only in my dreams.

Chorus 1

        F♯m7   G♯7   C♯m7
And I can   change _____ the world.

D♯m7♭5   G♯7   C♯m7
I would be the sun - light in your universe.

D♯m7♭5   G♯7   C♯m7   Cm7   Bm7
You would think my love __ was really some - thin' _ good,

     A*   Eadd2/G♯
Baby, if I could

E/G♯   E°7/G   F♯m11
Change _____ the world.

Interlude

| E F♯m7   Gadd9 | |
| F♯m7   E | |

Verse 2

    E   A/E   E7(no3rd)
   If I could be king,

     A/E E
Even for a day,

       A/E   E7(no 3rd)
I'd take you as my queen,

      A/E   E
I'd have it no other way.

A   D/A   A7(no 3rd)
  And our love would rule

        D/A   A
In this kingdom we have made.

E   A/E E7(no 3rd)
  Till then I'd be a fool,

      A/E   G♯7
Wishin' for the day...

Chorus 2

       F#m7   **G#7**   **C#m7**
And I can   change _____ the world.

D#m7b5   **G#7**   **C#m7**
I would be the sun - light in your universe.

D#m7b5   **G#7**   **C#m7**   **Cm7**   **Bm7**
You would think my love ____ was really some - thin' __ good,

     A **Eadd2/G#**
Baby, if I could

E/G#   **E°7/G** **F#m7**   **E**   **A/E**
Change _____ the world.

    E   **A7** **Eadd2/G#** **E/G#**   **E°7/G**   **F#m7**
Ba - by, if I could   change _____ the world.

Guitar Solo

E F#m7 Gadd9	
F#m7 E	
F#m7 Gadd9	
F#m7 G#7	

Chorus 3

       F#m7   **G#7**   **C#m7**
I could   change _____ the world.

D#m7b5   **G#7**   **C#m7**
I would be the sun - light in your universe.

D#m7b5   **G#7**   **C#m7**   **Cm7**   **Bm7**
You would think my love ____ was really some - thin' __ good,

      A* **Eadd2/G#**   **E/G#**   **E°7/G** **F#m11**
Baby, if I could   change the __ world,

      A* **Eadd2/G#**   **E/G#**   **E°7/G** **F#m11**
Baby, if I could   change the __ world,

      A* **Eadd2/G#**   **E/G#**   **E°7/G** **Gadd9**
Baby, if I could   change _____ the world.

Outro

| E   F#m7   Gadd9 | | F#m7 | E |

Could You Be Loved

Words and Music by Bob Marley

Melody:

Could you be loved? _____

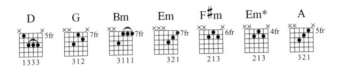

D   G   Bm   Em   F#m   Em*   A

Intro   ‖: N.C.(Bm)   :‖ *Play 6 times*

                           D
Chorus 1   Could you be loved?

                           G   **D**
                           Then be loved.

                           Could you be loved?

                           G   **D**
                           Then be loved.

                           Bm   **Em**
Verse 1   Don't let them fool ya,

                           Bm   **Em**
                           Or even try to school ya.

                           Oh, no.

                           Bm
                           We've got a mind of our own.

                                G   **F#m**   **Em***
                           So, go to hell if what   you thinkin' is not right.

                           Bm
                           Love would never leave us alone.

                                G   **F#m**   **A**
                           Ah, in the darkness, there must come out to light.

	D **Bm**

Chorus 2

    D   **Bm**
Could you be loved?

    G   **D**
Then be loved.

                          Bm
Now, could you be loved?

           G
Whoa,__ yeah.

           D   **Bm**
Then be loved.

Verse 2

Bm
Could you be loved, now, could you be loved?

The road of life is rocky and you may stumble too.

So, why don't you point your fingers at someone else that's judging you.

(Could you be, could you be, could you be loved?)

(Could you be, could you be loved?)

(Could you be, could you be, could you be loved?)

(Could you be, could you be loved?)

Verse 3

Bm   Em

Don't let them change ya, oh,

Bm

Or even rearrange ya.

Em

Oh, no.

Bm

We've got the life to live.

G   F♯m Em*

(Ooh, ooh, ooh.)

         Bm

They say   only, only,

        G   F♯m   A

Only the fittest of the fittest shall survive.

Stay alive. Eh.

Chorus 3

D   Bm

Could you be loved?

G   D

Then be loved.

                  Bm

Now, could you be loved?

        G   D

Whoa, __ yeah. Then be loved.

Outro

Bm

(Ain't gonna miss the water until the well runs dry.)

(And no matter how you treat the man, he'll never be satisfied.)

‖: Say something. Say something. :‖ *Repeat and fade (w/ voc. ad lib.)*

Come to My Window

Words and Music by Melissa Etheridge

Melody:

Come to my win - dow. _

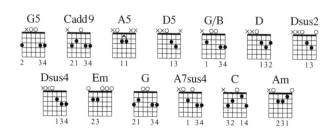

G5   Cadd9   A5   D5   G/B   D   Dsus2

Dsus4   Em   G   A7sus4   C   Am

Intro

G5   Cadd9   A5   D5
Come to my win - dow.

G5   Cadd9   A5   D5   G5
Crawl in-side, wait ____ by the light ____ of the moon.

        Cadd9   A5
Come to my win - dow,

D5
I'll be home soon.

Cadd9 G/B	D Dsus2 D Dsus2	Cadd9 G/B
Dsus2 D Dsus2 Dsus2	Cadd9 G/B
D Dsus2 D Dsus2	Cadd9 G/B	D Dsus2

Verse 1

Cadd9   G/B
I would dial the numbers

         D   Dsus4 D Dsus2
Just to lis - ten to your breath.

     Cadd9   G/B
And I would stand in-side my hell

         D   Dsus2 D Dsus2
And hold ____ the hand of death.

Cadd9   G/B
You don't know how far I'd go

  D   Dsus4 D Dsus2
To ease this precious ache.

     Cadd9   G/B
And you don't know how much I'd give

   D
Or how much I can take.

Pre-Chorus 1

       Em   Cadd9
Just to reach ____ you.

       D
Just to reach ____ you.

Dsus4 D   Em   Cadd9 D Dsus2 D Dsus2
Oh, ____ to ____ reach you, _____ oh.

Chorus 1

G   Cadd9 A7sus4   D Dsus2 D Dsus2
Come to my win - dow.

G   Cadd9
Crawl in-side,

  A7sus4   D   Dsus2 D Dsus2
Wait ____ by the light ____ of ____ the__ moon.

G   Cadd9 A7sus4
Come to my win - dow,

   D Dsus2   D Dsus2 G   Cadd9 A7sus4 D Dsus2 D Dsus2
I'll ____ be__ home _____ soon.

Verse 2

Cadd9   **G/B**
Keeping my eyes open

        Dsus4 Dsus2 D Dsus4   D Dsus2
I cannot ____ af - ford to ____ sleep.

Cadd9   **G/B**
Giving away promises

       D   **Dsus4**   **D Dsus2**
I know __ that I can't ____ keep.

Cadd9   **G/B**
Nothing fills the blackness

        Dsus2 D Dsus2 Dsus4 D Dsus2
That has seeped _____ into my   chest.

 Cadd9   **G/B**
I need you in my ___ blood

        D   **Dsus4 D Dsus4 D**
I am forsak - ing all the rest.

Pre-Chorus 2   *Repeat Pre-Chorus 1*

Chorus 2

G   **Cadd9** **A7sus4**   **D Dsus2 D Dsus2**
Come to my win - dow.

G   **Cadd9**
Crawl in-side,

  A7sus4   **D**   **Dsus2 D Dsus2**
Wait ____ by the light __ of ____ the__ moon.

G   **Cadd9** **A7sus4**
Come to my win - dow,

   D **Dsus2**   **D Dsus2 G**   **Cadd9** **A7sus4 D**
I'll __ be___ home _____ soon.

Bridge

Em
I don't care what they think.

C
I don't care what they say.

Am
What do they know about this love,

D Dsus4 D   Dsus2   Dsus4   D
Any - way?

Interlude

| G   Cadd9 |A7sus4 Dsus4 D Dsus2 D Dsus2 |
| G   Cadd9 |A7sus4   Dsus4 |

     Cadd9   G/B   D   Dsus2 D
Come, ____ come __ to my win-dow,

Dsus4 D Dsus2   Cadd9
I'll   be home, I'll ____ be home,

  G/B   D   Dsus2
I'll ____ be home.   I'm comin' home.

Chorus 3

G   Cadd9 A7sus4
Come to my win - dow.

D Dsus2 D G   Cadd9
Oh, _____   crawl in-side,

  A7sus4   D   Dsus2 D   G
Wait ___ by the light ___ of the ___ moon.

    Cadd9   A7sus4
Come to my win - dow,

  D   Dsus2   G
I'll ___ be home soon,

  Cadd9   A7sus4
I'll ___ be home, I'll____ be home,

   D   Dsus2
I'm comin' home.

Chorus 4   *Repeat Chorus 3*

Outro   ‖: G   Cadd9 | A7sus4 D Dsus2 :‖ *Repeat and fade*

Crazy Little Thing Called Love

Words and Music by Freddie Mercury

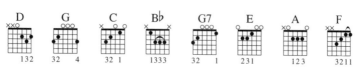

Verse 1

          D
This thing___ called love,

      G   **C**   **G**
I just__ can't handle it.

         D
This thing,___ called love,

     G   **C**   **G**
I must__ get 'round to it.

      D
I ain't ready.

Bb   **C**   **D**
Crazy little thing called love.

Verse 2

         D
This thing___ (This thing.) called love, (Called love.)

    G   **C**   **G**
It cries__ (Like a baby.) in a cradle all night.

       D
It swings,___ (Woo, woo.) it jives, (Woo,woo.)

    G   **C**   **G**
It shakes__ all over like a jellyfish.

      D
I kinda like it.

Bb   **C**   **D**
Crazy little thing called love.

Bridge 1

        G7
There goes my baby,

   C   **G**
She knows how to rock 'n' roll.

       Bb
She drives me crazy.

      E   **A**
She gives me hot and cold fever,

     F   **N.C.**   **E**
Then she leaves me in a cool, cool sweat.

Verse 3

 A   **D**
   I gotta be cool,__ relax,

  G **C**   **G**
Get hip,__ get on my tracks,

   D
Take the back seat, hitch hike,

 G   **C**   **G**
And take a long ride on my motor-bike

   D
Until I'm ready.

Bb   **C**   **D**
Crazy little thing called love.

Bridge 2   ***Repeat Bridge 1***

Verse 4   ***Repeat Verse 3***

Verse 5   ***Repeat Verse 1***

Outro

      Bb   **C**   **D**
‖: Crazy little thing called love. :‖ ***Repeat and fade***

Daydream

Words and Music by John Sebastian

Melody:

What a day for a day - dream,

(Capo 1st fret)

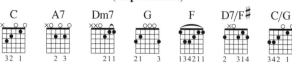

C   A7   Dm7   G   F   D7/F#   C/G

Intro
```
| C      |      |      |
```

Verse 1

    C   A7
What a day for a day - dream,
Dm7   **G**
What a day for a daydreamin' boy.
    C   A7
And I'm lost in a day - dream,
Dm7   **G**
Dreamin' 'bout my bundle of joy.

Bridge 1

  F   **D7/F#**   **C/G**   **A7**
And even if time ain't really on my side,
  F   **D7/F#**   **C/G**   **A7**
It's one of those days for taking a walk outside.
  F   **D7/F#**   **C/G**   **A7**
I'm blowing the day to take a walk in the sun,
  G
And fall on my face on somebody's new mown lawn.

Verse 2

    C   A7
I've been having a sweet ___ dream,
Dm7   **G**
I've been dreamin' since I woke up today.
    C   A7
It's starring me and my sweet ___ dream,
Dm7   **G**
'Cause she's the one makes me feel this way.

Bridge 2

    F   D7/F♯   C/G   A7
And even if time is passing by a lot,

    F   D7/F♯   C/G   A7
I couldn't care less about the dues you say I ___ got.

    F   D7/F♯   C/G   A7
Tomorrow I'll pay the dues for dropping my load,

    G
A pie in the face for being a sleepy bull toad.

Interlude

‖: C | A7 | Dm7 | G   :‖

Verse 3

    F   D7/F♯   C/G   A7
And you can be sure that if you're feelin' right,

    F   D7/F♯   C/G   A7
A daydream will last till long into the night.

    F   D7/F♯   C/G   A7
Tomorrow at breakfast you may pick up your ears,

    G
Or you may be daydreamin' for a thousand years.

Verse 4

    C   A7
What a day for a day - dream,

    Dm7   G
Custom made for a daydreamin' boy.

    C   A7
Now, I'm lost in a day - dream,

    Dm7   G
Dreamin' 'bout my bundle of joy.

Outro

‖: F   D7/F♯ | C/G   A7 :‖ *Repeat and fade*

Don't Stop

Words and Music by Christine McVie

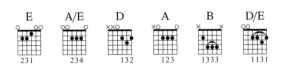

E	A/E	D	A	B	D/E
231	234	132	123	1333	1131

Intro

‖: E   A/E │ E   A/E │ E   A/E │ E   A/E :‖

Verse 1

   E   D   A
If you wake up and don't want to smile;

   E   D   A
If it takes just a little while,

   E   D   A
Open your eyes and look at the day.

   B
You'll see things in a diff'rent way.

Chorus 1

   E   D/E A
Don't stop   thinking about tomorrow.

   E   D/E A
Don't stop.   It'll soon be here.

   E   D/E A
It'll be ____ better than before.

   B
Yesterday's gone. Yesterday's gone.

Interlude

│ E   D │ A │ E   D │ A │

Verse 2

```
        E       D      A
Why not think about times to come,

        E         D      A
And not a-bout the things that you've done.

        E      D     A
If your life was bad to you,

        B
Just think what tomorrow will do.
```

Chorus 2   *Repeat Chorus 1*

Guitar Solo

```
|E    D  |A        |E    D  |A          |
|E    D  |A        |B        |          |
|        |         |         |
```

Verse 3

```
        E     D      A
All I want is to see you smile,

        E    D        A
If it takes just a little while.

        E          D        A
I know you don't be-lieve that it's true.

        B
I never meant any harm to you.
```

Chorus 3

```
        E    D/E  A
Don't stop   thinking about tomorrow.

        E    D/E  A N.C.
Don't stop.  It'll soon be here.

        E        D/E   A
It'll be ____ better than before.

        B
Yesterday's gone. Yesterday's gone.
```

Chorus 4   *Repeat Chorus 1*

Outro

```
        E   D/E  A                  E     D/E  A
||:  Ooh, ____ don't you look back.              :|| Repeat and fade
```

Drive

Words and Music by Brandon Boyd,
Michael Einziger, Alex Katunich,
Jose Pasillas II and Chris Kilmore

Melody:

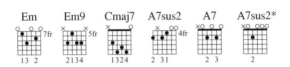

Some-times   I   feel _ the   fear _ of ___

Em   Em9   Cmaj7   A7sus2   A7   A7sus2*

Intro ‖: Em   Em9 | Cmaj7   A7sus2 :‖ *Play 4 times*

Verse 1

Em   Em9 Cmaj7   A7sus2
Sometimes   I feel the fear of

Em   Em9 Cmaj7 A7sus2
Un-certainty stinging clear.

Em   Em9   Cmaj7
And I,   I can't help but ask myself

A7sus2   Em   Em9   Cmaj7   A7sus2
How much I'll let the fear take the wheel ___ and steer.

Pre-Chorus 1

Cmaj7   A7
It's driven me be-fore,

A7sus2* A7 A7sus2* Cmaj7
And it seems to have ___ a vague,

A7   A7sus2* A7 A7sus2* Cmaj7
Haunting mass ap - peal.

A7   A7sus2* A7
But lately I'm beginning to   find ___ that

A7sus2* Cmaj7   A7
I _____ should be the one behind the wheel.

Chorus 1

```
Em          Em9 Cmaj7            A7sus2 Em
Whatever tomor  -  row brings, I'll    be ___ there
```

```
     Em9      Cmaj7              A7sus2
With open arms ___ and open eyes, ___ yeah.
```

```
Em          Em9 Cmaj7            A7sus2 Em
Whatever tomor  -  row brings, I'll    be ___ there,
```

```
Em9    Cmaj7   A7sus2
I'll be ___  there.
```

Verse 2

```
Em    Em9    Cmaj7          A7sus2
So if I    de-cide to waiver my
```

```
       Em              Em9   Cmaj7   A7sus2
Chance to be one of the hive,
```

```
Em    Em9    Cmaj7          A7sus2
Will I   choose water over wine
```

```
        Em
And hold my own and drive?
```

```
   Em9 Cmaj7  A7sus2
Oh, oh,   oh.
```

Pre-Chorus 2

```
Cmaj7              A7
It's driven me be-fore,
```

```
         A7sus2* A7  A7sus2*  Cmaj7
And it seems to have ___ a vague,
```

```
A7           A7sus2* A7  A7sus2* Cmaj7
Haunting mass ap  -    peal.
```

```
     A7              A7sus2* A7
But lately I'm beginning to find _____
```

```
     A7sus2* Cmaj7        A7
That when _____ I drive my-self my light is found.
```

Chorus 2	*Repeat Chorus 1*
Interlude	*Repeat Intro*

Pre-Chorus 3	**Cmaj7** **A7** **Cmaj7** Would you choose a, water over wine? **A7** **N.C.** Hold the wheel and drive.

Chorus 3	*Repeat Chorus 1*

Outro

Em   **Em9**   **Cmaj7**   **A7sus2**
Do, do, do, ____ do, do, do,

        Em
Do, do, do, ____ do.

Em9   **Cmaj7**
No, no, ____ no.

    A7sus2   **Em**
Do, do, do, do, do.

     Em9   **Cmaj7**   **A7sus2**
Do, do, do, do, ____ do, do, do,

        Em
Do, do, do, ____ do.

Em9   **Cmaj7**   **A7sus2**   **Cmaj7**   **A7**
No, no, __ no, no, no.

Fast Car

Words and Music by Tracy Chapman

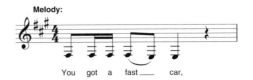

(Capo 2nd fret)

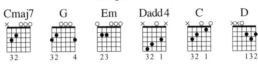

Intro ‖: Cmaj7 G |Em Dadd4 :‖ *Play 4 times*

Verse 1

Cmaj7   G
You got a fast __ car,

Em   Dadd4
I want a ticket ____ to anywhere.

Cmaj7   G
Maybe we make a deal,

Em   Dadd4
Maybe together we can get somewhere.

Cmaj7   G
Anyplace is better.

Em   Dadd4
Starting from zero, got nothing to lose.

Cmaj7   G
Maybe we'll make something;

Em   Dadd4
Me, myself, I got nothing to prove.

| *Interlude 1* | ‖: Cmaj7   G |Em   Dadd4   :‖ |

Verse 2

     Cmaj7   G
You got a fast __ car,

     Em   Dadd4
I got a plan ____ to get us out of here.

         Cmaj7   G
I been working at the con-venience store,

     Em   Dadd4
Managed to save just a little bit of money.

     Cmaj7   G
Won't have to drive too far,

         Em   Dadd4
Just 'cross the border and into the city.

     Cmaj7   G
You and I can both get jobs

         Em   Dadd4
And finally see what it means to be living.

Interlude 2   *Repeat Interlude 1*

Verse 3

         Cmaj7   G
You see, my old man's got a problem.

         Em   Dadd4
He live with the bottle, that's the way it is.

         Cmaj7   G
He says his body's too old for working;

         Em   Dadd4
His body's too young ____ to look like his.

         Cmaj7   G
My mama went off and left him;

         Em   Dadd4
She wanted more from life than he could give.

         Cmaj7   G
I said somebody's got to take care of him.

         Em   Dadd4
So I quit school and that's what I did.

Interlude 3   *Repeat Interlude 1*

Verse 4
```
Cmaj7      G
```
You got a fast __ car,
```
        Em          Dadd4
```
But is it fast enough so we can fly away?
```
Cmaj7      G
```
We gotta make a decision:
```
Em              Dadd4
```
Leave tonight or live and die this way.
```
|Cmaj7    G  |Em    Dadd4  |Cmaj7    G      |
Em       Dadd4
```
   'Cause I remember when we were...

Chorus 1
```
C
```
Driving, driving in your car,
```
      G
```
The speed so fast I felt like I was drunk.
```
Em
```
   City lights lay out before us
```
         D
```
And your arm felt nice wrapped 'round my shoulder.
```
       C  Em    D
```
And I,   I had a feeling that I belonged.
```
C  Em    D
```
I,   I had a feeling I could be someone,
```
C           D
```
Be someone,   be someone.

Interlude 4   *Repeat Interlude 1*

Verse 5

Cmaj7   G
You got a fast __ car.

Em   Dadd4
We go cruising to entertain ourselves.

   Cmaj7   G
You still ain't got a job

     Em   Dadd4
And I work in a market as a checkout girl.

Cmaj7   G
I know things will get better;

Em   Dadd4
You'll find work and I'll get promoted.

Cmaj7   G
We'll move out of the shelter,

Em   Dadd4
Buy a big house and live in the suburbs.

| Cmaj7 G | Em Dadd4 | Cmaj7 G | |

Em   Dadd4
  'Cause I remember when we were...

Chorus 2   *Repeat Chorus 1*

Interlude 5   *Repeat Interlude 1*

Verse 6

Cmaj7   G
You got a fast ___ car.

Em   Dadd4
I got a job that pays all our bills.

Cmaj7   G
You stay out drinking   late at the bar;

Em   Dadd4
See more of your friends than you do of your kids.

Cmaj7   G
I'd always hoped for better;

Em   Dadd4
Thought maybe together   you and me'd find it.

Cmaj7   G
I got no plans, I ain't going nowhere,

Em   Dadd4
So take your fast car and keep on driving.

|Cmaj7   G |Em   Dadd4 |Cmaj7   G |

Em   Dadd4
'Cause I remember when we were...

Chorus 3   *Repeat Chorus 1*

Interlude 6   *Repeat Interlude 1*

Verse 7

Cmaj7   G
You got a fast ___ car.

Em   Dadd4
Is it fast enough so you can fly away?

Cmaj7   G
You gotta make a decision:

Em   Dadd4
Leave tonight or live and die this way.

Outro   ‖: Cmaj7   G |Em   Dadd4 :‖ *Play 3 times*
             | Cmaj7   G

Dust in the Wind

Words and Music by Kerry Livgren

Melody:

I close my eyes, _____

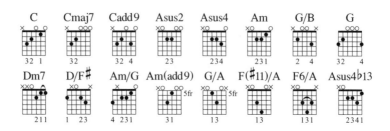

Intro

C	Cmaj7	Cadd9	C	Asus2	Asus4
Am	Asus2	Cadd9	C	Cmaj7	Cadd9
Am	Asus2	Asus4	Am G/B		

Verse 1

    C G/B Am
I close my eyes,

G   Dm7   Am   G/B
Only for a mo - ment, and the mo - ment's gone.

C G/B Am
All my dreams

G   Dm7   Am
Pass before my eyes, ____ a curi-osity.

Chorus 1

D/F♯   G   Am Am/G
Dust ____ in the wind.

D/F♯   G   Am   G/B
All they are is dust in the wind.

Verse 2

```
C    G/B Am
Same old  song.

G              Dm7          Am
Just a drop of wa - ter in an end - less sea.

C G/B Am
All  we  do

G                    Dm7          Am
Crumbles to the ground __ though we re-fuse to see.
```

Chorus 2

```
D/F♯   G      Am  Am/G
  Dust __in the wind.

D/F♯       G        Am(add9)   G/A
All we are is dust in the wind.

F(♯11)/A  F6/A  F(♯11)/A
Oh, ho,    ho.
```

Interlude 1   ‖: Am(add9) │G/A   │F(♯11)/A │F6/A F(♯11)/A :‖

Interlude 2   *Repeat Intro*

Verse 3

```
G/B C   G/B Am
Now don't hang on,

G              Dm7          Am
Nothing lasts forev - er but the earth __ and sky.

G/B C   G/B Am
It   slips a - way

    G          Dm7          Am
And all your money won't another minute buy.
```

Chorus 3

```
D/F♯  G      Am  Am/G
  Dust __ in the wind.

D/F♯       G          Am  Am/G
All we are is dust in the wind.

D/F♯  G      Am      Am/G
  Dust __ in the wind.

D/F♯      G        Am
Ev'rything is dust in the wind.
```

Outro   ‖: Am Asus2 │Asus4♭13 Am│Asus2 Asus4♭13 :‖ *Repeat and fade*

Fields of Gold

Music and Lyrics by Sting

Melody:

You'll re - mem - ber me

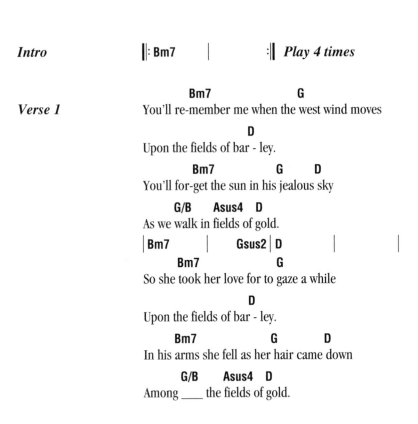

Bm7   G   D   G/B   Asus4   Gsus2

Intro   ‖: Bm7 | :‖ *Play 4 times*

Verse 1

            Bm7   G
You'll re-member me when the west wind moves

                D
Upon the fields of bar - ley.

          Bm7   G   D
You'll for-get the sun in his jealous sky

         G/B   Asus4   D
As we walk in fields of gold.

  Bm7 | Gsus2 | D | |
          Bm7   G
So she took her love for to gaze a while

                D
Upon the fields of bar - ley.

        Bm7   G   D
In his arms she fell as her hair came down

         G/B   Asus4   D
Among ____ the fields of gold.

GUITAR CHORD SONGBOOK

Verse 2

```
            Bm7                 G
Will you stay with me, will you be my love
                  D
Among the fields of bar - ley?
            Bm7           G     D
We'll for-get the sun in his jealous sky
         G/B  Asus4  D
As we lie in fields of gold.
|Bm7          |       Gsus2| D        |          |
         Bm7                 G
See the west wind move like a lover so
                  D
Upon the fields of bar - ley.
            Bm7           G     D
Feel her body rise when you kiss her mouth
         G/B      Asus4   D
Among ____ the fields of gold.
```

Bridge

```
Gsus2         D
   I never made promises lightly
Gsus2               D
   And there have been some that I've broken,
Gsus2            D
   But I swear in the days still left
         G/B      Asus4   D
We'll walk ____ in fields of gold.
         G/B      Asus4  D
We'll walk in fields of gold.
```

Guitar Solo	|Bm7	|G			|D		
	|Bm7	|G D	|G/B Asus4 |D	

Bm7   **G**

Verse 3

Many years have passed since those __ summer days

               D

Among the fields of bar - ley.

    Bm7   **G**   **D**

See the children run as the sun goes down

   G/B   **Asus4** **D**

Among ___ the fields of gold.

    Bm7   **G**

You'll re-member me when the west wind moves

          D

Upon the fields of bar - ley.

    Bm7   **G**   **D**

You can tell the sun in his jealous sky

D   **G/B**   **Asus4** **D**

When we walked in fields of gold.

    G/B   **Asus4** **D**

When we walked in fields of gold,

    G/B   **Asus4** **D**

When we walked in fields of gold.

Outro

‖: D   Gsus2 D :‖ *Play 7 times*

|D

Iris

from the Motion Picture CITY OF ANGELS

Words and Music by John Rzeznik

Tuning:
(low to high) B-D-D-D-D-D

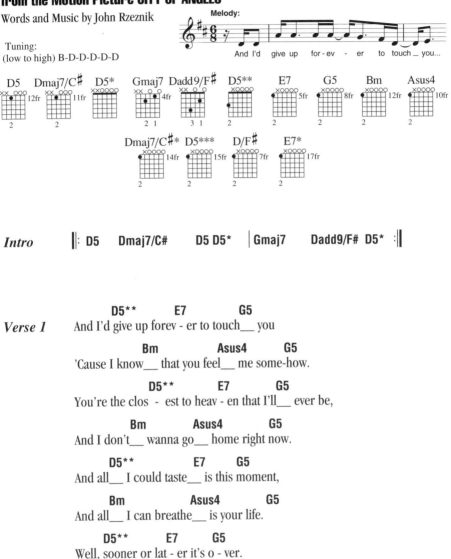

Intro ‖: D5   Dmaj7/C#   D5 D5* | Gmaj7   Dadd9/F# D5* :‖

Verse 1

    D5** E7   G5
And I'd give up forev - er to touch__ you

    Bm   Asus4 G5
'Cause I know__ that you feel__ me some-how.

    D5** E7   G5
You're the clos - est to heav - en that I'll__ ever be,

    Bm   Asus4 G5
And I don't__ wanna go__ home right now.

    D5** E7 G5
And all__ I could taste__ is this moment,

    Bm   Asus4 G5
And all__ I can breathe__ is your life.

    D5** E7 G5
Well, sooner or lat - er it's o - ver.

    Bm   Asus4   G5
I just don't__ wanna miss__ you tonight.

Chorus 1

          Bm   **Asus4**   **G5**
And I don't want the world__ to see__ me

                Bm   **Asus4**   **G5**
'Cause I don't__ think that they'd__ under-stand.

       Bm   **Asus4**   **G5**
When everything's made to be bro - ken

           Bm   **Asus4**   **G5**
I just want__ you to know__ who I am.

Interlude 1   ***Repeat Intro***

Verse 2

             D5**   **E7**   **G5**
And you can't__ fight the tears__ that ain't comin',

       Bm   **Asus4**   **G5**
Or the mo - ment of truth__ in your lies.

       D5**   **E7**   **G5**
When ev'rything feels like the mov - ies,

            Bm   **Asus4**   **G5**
Yeah, you bleed__ just to know__ you're alive.

Chorus 2   ***Repeat Chorus 1***

Interlude 2 ‖: Bm Dmaj7/C#* | D5*** | Bm Asus4 | G5 :‖
‖: Bm Dmaj7/C#* D5*** | G5 :‖ *Play 4 times*
| D/F# | G5 | Bm | G5 |
| D/F# | Bm |
| Dmaj7/C#* D5*** E7* D5*** Dmaj7/C#* |
| G5 | D/F# | Bm | |
‖: Bm Dmaj7/C#* | D5*** | Bm Asus4 | G5 :‖

Chorus 3 **Repeat Chorus 1**

Chorus 4 **Repeat Chorus 1**

          Bm   Asus4   G5
Outro I just want__ you to know__ who I am.

          Bm   Asus4   G5
I just want__ you to know__ who I am.

          Bm   Asus4   G5
I just want__ you to know__ who I am.

          Bm   Asus4   Bm
I just want__ you to know__ who I am.

‖: Bm Dmaj7/C#* | D5*** | Bm Asus4 | G5 :‖ *Repeat and fade*

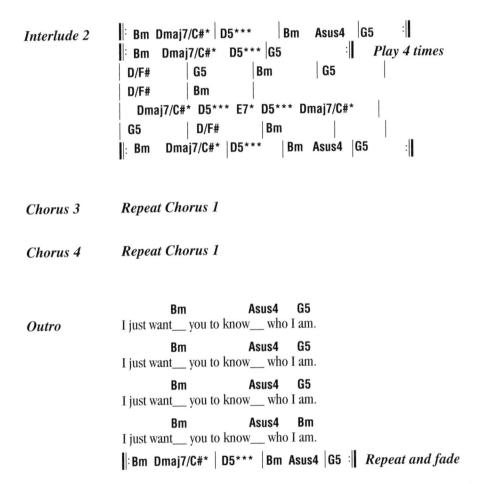

Give a Little Bit

Words and Music by Rick Davies
and Roger Hodgson

Melody:

Give a lit - tle bit, _____

D   G   A   Bm   E7   Bm/A   F#7   Gmaj7   C

Verse 1

    D
Give a little bit,

            G   **A**   **G A** **G**
Give a little bit of your love__ to me.

    D   **A**
I'll give a little bit,

    D   **G**   **A**   **G A** **G**
I'll give a little bit of my love__ to you.

Bm   **E7**
There's so much that we need__ to share,

   G   **Bm/A A**   **D** **A**
So send a smile and show__ you care.

Verse 2

    D   **A**
I'll give a little bit,

    D   **G**   **A**   **G** **A** **G**
I'll give a little bit of my life__ for you.

    D   **A**
So, give a little bit,

    D   **G**   **A**   **G** **A** **G**
Oh, give a little bit of your time__ to me.

Bm   **E7**
See the man with the lone - ly eyes?

   G   **Bm/A A**   **D** **A**
Oh, take his hand, you'll be sur - prised.

Solo   ‖: F#7 | Gmaj7   :‖
          | C   G | A   D | A | D | A |

Verse 3
D
          Give a little bit,

                    G   **A**   **G A**   **G**
          Give a little bit of your love__ to me.

D   **A**
          I'll give a little bit,

D   **G**   **A**   **G A**   **G**
          I'll give a little bit of my life__ to you.

Bm   **E7**
          Now's the time that we need__ to share,

          G
          So find yourself,

               C   **G**   **A**   **D**
          We're on our way back home.

A   **D**   **A**   **D**
          Oh,__ goin' home.

A   **D**   **A**   **D**
          Don't you need, don't you need to feel at home?

A   **D**   **G** **A** **G** **D**
          Oh, yeah,__ we gotta sing.

Have You Ever Really Loved a Woman?
from the Motion Picture DON JUAN DeMARCO

Words and Music by Bryan Adams,
Michael Kamen and Robert John Lange

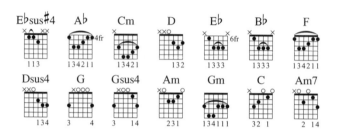

Intro | E♭sus♯4 | A♭   Cm | D |

                                      E♭

Verse 1   To really love a wom - an,

                          Cm
                     To under-stand her

                          D
                     You got to know her deep inside.

                          B♭
                     Hear ev'ry thought, see ev'ry dream

                          F
                     And give her wings when she wants to fly.

                          Cm
                     Then when you find yourself

                          Dsus4   **D**
                     Lying helpless in her arms.

Chorus 1

```
        G       D     Gsus4 G
```
You know you really love a woman.

```
                                              D
```
When you love a woman you tell her she's really want - ed.

```
                                          G
```
When you love a woman you tell her that she's the one.

'Cause she needs somebody to tell her

```
                      Am  D      Am    D
```
That it's gonna last_____ for-ever.

```
   Am                 D
```
So tell me have you ever really,

```
   Am              D      G
```
Really, really ever loved a woman? Yeah.

Verse 2

```
                      Gm
```
To really love a woman,

```
          Cm
```
Let her hold you

```
          D
```
Till you know how she needs to be touched.

```
              Bb               Am
```
You got to breathe her, really taste her

```
   Gm         F
```
Till you can feel her in your blood.

```
                      Eb
```
And when you can see

```
                      Dsus4  D
```
Your unborn children in her eyes.

Chorus 2

       E♭   D   Gsus4   G
You know you really   love a woman.

When you love a woman

                  D
You tell her she's really want - ed. Yeah.

When you love a woman

             G
You tell her that she's the one.

'Cause she needs somebody to tell her

          Am   D   Am   D
That you'll always be _____ togeth - er.

  Am   D
So tell me have you ever really,

  Am   D   G
Really, really ever loved a woman?

Bridge

               E♭
Oh, you've got to give her some faith,

              G
Hold her tight, a little tenderness,

You got to treat her right.

D
She will be there for you;

             G
Taking good care of you.

You really got to love your woman, yeah.

Guitar Solo		Eb		Cm	D		Bb F	
		Bb		F	Am	F		

Interlude

           Cm
And when you find yourself

                  Dsus4 D
Lying helpless in her arms

                Gsus4   G
You know you really love a wom-an.

Chorus 3

           G
When you love a woman

                     D
You tell her that she's really want - ed.

When you love a woman

                G
You tell her that she's the one. Yeah.

'Cause she needs somebody to tell her

           Am D   **Am D**
That it's gonna last _____ for-ever.

   Am   **D**
So tell me have you ever really,

Am   **D**   **G**
Really, really ever loved a woman? Yeah.

   C   **D**
Just tell me have you ever really,

C   **D**   **G**
Really, really ever loved a woman?

     C   **D**
Oh, just tell me have you ever really,

Am7   **D**   **G**
Really, really ever loved a woman?

Here Comes the Sun

Words and Music by George Harrison

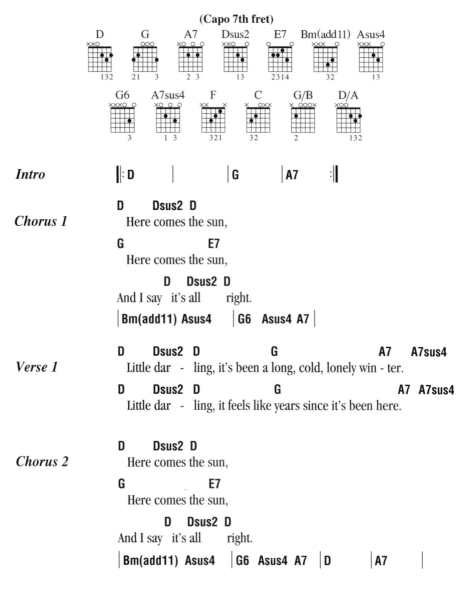

Intro

‖: D | | G | A7 :‖

Chorus 1

D　　Dsus2　D
Here comes the sun,

G　　　　　　　E7
Here comes the sun,

　　　　　　D　　Dsus2　D
And I say　it's all　　　right.

|Bm(add11)　Asus4　|G6　Asus4　A7 |

Verse 1

D　　Dsus2　D　　　　　　　　G　　　　　　　　　A7　　A7sus4
Little dar　-　ling, it's been a long, cold, lonely win - ter.

D　　Dsus2　D　　　　　　　　G　　　　　　　　A7　　A7sus4
Little dar　-　ling, it feels like years since it's been here.

Chorus 2

D　　Dsus2　D
Here comes the sun,

G　　　　　　　　E7
Here comes the sun,

　　　　　　D　　Dsus2　D
And I say　it's all　　　right.

|Bm(add11)　Asus4　|G6　Asus4　A7　|D　　|A7　　　|

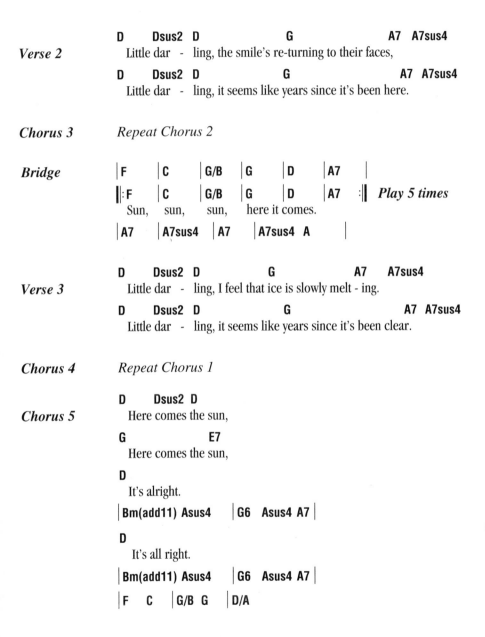

| | D   Dsus2 D | G | A7 A7sus4 |

Verse 2
   D   Dsus2 D   G   A7 A7sus4
   Little dar - ling, the smile's re-turning to their faces,

   D   Dsus2 D   G   A7 A7sus4
   Little dar - ling, it seems like years since it's been here.

Chorus 3   *Repeat Chorus 2*

Bridge | F | C | G/B | G | D | A7 |
           ||: F | C | G/B | G | D | A7 :|| *Play 5 times*
           Sun,   sun,   sun,   here it comes.
           | A7 | A7sus4 | A7 | A7sus4 A |

Verse 3
   D   Dsus2 D   G   A7 A7sus4
   Little dar - ling, I feel that ice is slowly melt - ing.

   D   Dsus2 D   G   A7 A7sus4
   Little dar - ling, it seems like years since it's been clear.

Chorus 4   *Repeat Chorus 1*

Chorus 5
   D   Dsus2 D
   Here comes the sun,

   G   E7
   Here comes the sun,

   D
   It's alright.
   | Bm(add11) Asus4 | G6 Asus4 A7 |

   D
   It's all right.
   | Bm(add11) Asus4 | G6 Asus4 A7 |
   | F   C | G/B G | D/A |

Here, There and Everywhere

Words and Music by
John Lennon and
Paul McCartney

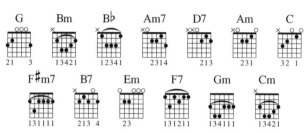

Intro

| G | Bm |
To lead a better life,

| Bb | | Am7 D7 |
I need my love to be here.

Verse 1

| G | Am |
Here,

| Bm | C | G | Am |
Making each day___ of the year.

| Bm | C | F#m7 | B7 |
Changing my life___ with a wave___ of her hand.

| F#m7 | B7 | Em | | Am | Am7 D7 |
Nobody can___ deny___ that there's some - thing there.

Verse 2

| G | Am |
There,

| Bm | C | G | Am |
Running my hands___ through her hair.

| Bm | C | F#m7 | B7 |
Both of us think - ing how good___ it can be.

| F#m7 | B7 | Em | | Am | Am7 D7 |
Someone is speak-ing, but she doesn't know___ he's there.

Bridge 1

F7   Bb   Gm
I want her ev'rywhere,

        Cm   D7   Gm
And if she's beside me, I know I need never care.

Cm   D7
But to love her is to need her

Verse 3

G   Am
Ev'rywhere.

Bm   C   G   Am
Knowing that love__ is to share.

Bm   C   F#m7   B7
Each one believ - ing that love__ never dies,

F#m7   B7   Em   Am   Am7 D7
Watching their eyes__ and hoping I'm al - ways there.

Bridge 2

F7   Bb   Gm
I want her ev'rywhere,

        Cm   D7   Gm
And if she's beside me, I know I need never care.

Cm   D7
But to love her is to need her

Verse 4

G   Am
Ev'rywhere.

Bm   C   G   Am
Knowing that love__ is to share.

Bm   C   F#m7   B7
Each one believ - ing that love__ never dies.

F#m7   B7   Em   Am   Am7 D7
Watching her eyes__ and hoping I'm al - ways there.

        G   Am
I will be there

     Bm   C
And ev'rywhere.

G   Am   Bm   C   G
Here, there and ev'rywhere.

I'll Have to Say I Love You in a Song

Words and Music by Jim Croce

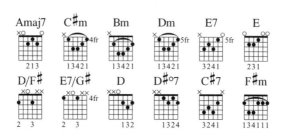

Intro

‖: Amaj7 | C♯m | Bm | Dm E7 :‖

Verse 1

     Amaj7   **C♯m**
Well, I know it's kind of late,

Bm   **E**
   I hope I didn't wake ___ ya.

D/F♯ E7/G♯ Amaj7   **C♯m**
   But what I gotta say can't wait.

Bm   **E**   **D/F♯ E7/G♯**
   I know you'd understand.

Chorus 1

   D   **D♯ 7**
   'Cause ev'ry time I tried to tell you

   C♯7   **F♯m** **D**
The words just came out wrong.

   Amaj7   **E**   **D** **Amaj7** **E**
So I'll have to say I love ___ ya in a song.

Verse 2

Amaj7   C#m
Yeah, I know it's kind of strange

Bm   E
 But ev'ry time I'm near __ ya,

D/F# E7/G# Amaj7   C#m
 I just run out of things to say.

Bm   E D/F# E7/G#
 I know you'd understand.

Chorus 2 *Repeat Chorus 1*

Guitar Solo ‖: Amaj7 | C#m | Bm | E D/F# E7/G# :‖

Chorus 3

D   D# 7
 'Cause ev'ry time ____ the time was right

 C#7   F#m D
All the words just came out wrong.

 Amaj7 E   D Amaj7 E
So I'll have to say I love __ ya in a song.

Verse 3

 Amaj7   C#m
Yeah, I know it's kind of late,

Bm   E
 I hope I didn't wake __ ya.

D/F# E7/G# Amaj7   C#m
 But there's somethin' that I just got to say,

Bm   E D/F# E7/G#
 I know you'd understand.

Chorus 4 *Repeat Chorus 1*

Outro ‖: Amaj7 | C#m | Bm | Dm E7 :‖
     | Amaj7

If You Could Only See

Words and Music by Emerson Hart

Melody:

If you could on - ly see ___ the ___ way ___

(Capo 1st fret)

Am   C/G   G5   G5/F   Asus2   Cmaj7/E   G6

Fmaj7#11   A5   Dadd4   Cmaj7   Em   E

	N.C.	Am		C/G

Chorus 1 If you could only see ___ the way she loves ___ me.

                            G5
Then maybe you would un - derstand

G5/F   **G5**   **Am**   **C/G**
Why I feel this way ___ about our love,

                 G5
And what I must do.

G5/F   **G5** **Am**
If you could on-ly see___ how blue

          C/G   **G5**
Her eyes ___ can be when she says,

G5/F
When she says she loves me.

Interlude 1   ‖: Asus2   Cmaj7/E |G6   Fmaj7#11 :‖

                 A5
Verse 1   Well, you got your reasons

Fmaj7#11   **Dadd4**
And you got your lies.

A5
And you got your manipulations,

Fmaj7#11   **Dadd4**
They cut me down to size.

Pre-Chorus 1

    Asus2   **Cmaj7**
Sayin' you love but you ___ don't.

                    G6
You give your love but you ___ won't.

Chorus 2

                   Am   **C/G**
If you could only see ___ the way she loves ___ me,

                 G5
Then maybe you would un - derstand

G5/F   **G5**   **Am**   **C/G**
  Why I feel this way ___ about our love,

              G5
And what I must do.

G5/F   **G5**   **Am**
  If you could on-ly see ___ how blue

         C/G   **G5**
Her eyes ___ can be when she says,

G5/F   **G5**   **Asus2**
  When she says ___ she loves ___ me.

Interlude 2

Repeat Interlude 1

Verse 2

A5
   Seems the road less traveled

Fmaj7♯11   **Dadd4**
  Shows happiness unrav - eled.

A5
   And you got to take a little dirt

             Fmaj7♯11
To keep what you love.

Dadd4
That's what you gotta do.

Pre-Chorus 2

Asus2   Cmaj7
Sayin' you love but you ____ don't.

         G6
You give your love but you ____ won't.

          Fmaj7♯11   G6
You're stretching out your arms____ to something that's just not there.

Asus2   Cmaj7
Sayin' you love where you ____ stand.

         G6
Give your heart when you ____ can.

Chorus 3

         Am   C/G
If you could only see ____ the way she loves ____ me,

         G5
Then maybe you would un - derstand

G5/F   G5   Am   C/G
Why I feel this way ____ about our love,

        G5
And what I must do.

G5/F   G5 Am
If you could on-ly see ____ how blue

      C/G   G5
Her eyes ____ can be when she says,

Em
When she says she loves me.

Guitar Solo ‖: E   Fmaj7♯11 │G5   Am :‖ *Play 4 times*

Pre-Chorus 3

Asus2   Cmaj7
Sayin' you love but you ___ don't.

         G6
You give your love but you ___ won't.

Fmaj7♯11 G6
Sayin',

Asus2   Cmaj7
Sayin' you love where you ___ stand.

       G6
Give your heart when you ___ can.

Chorus 4

        Am   C/G
If you could only see___ the way she loves ___ me,

         G5
Then maybe you would un - derstand

G5/F G5 Am   C/G
Why I feel this way ___ about our love,

       G5
And what I must do.

G5/F   G5 Am
If you could on-ly see ___ how blue

    C/G   G5
Her eyes ___ can be when she says,

Fmaj7♯11
When she says she loves me.

Jumper

Words and Music by
Stephan Jenkins

I wish you would step back from _ that ledge, __ my friend.

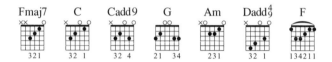

Fmaj7   C   Cadd9   G   Am   Dadd⁴₉   F

Chorus 1

> **Fmaj7**   **C**   **Cadd9**
> I wish you would step back
>
>   **G**
> From that ledge, ___ my friend.
>
>   **Fmaj7**   **C Cadd9**
> You could   cut ties with all the lies
>
>   **G**
> That you've ___ been living in.
>
>   **Fmaj7**   **C**   **Cadd9**   **G**
> And   if you do not want ___ to see me ___ again,
>
> **N.C.**   **Fmaj7** **C Cadd9** **G**
> I would under-stand,
>
>   **Fmaj7** **C Cadd9** **G**
> I would under-stand.

Verse 1

Am
The angry boy, a bit too insane,

C
Icing over a secret pain.

G
You know you don't belong.

Am
You're the first to fight, you're way too loud.

C
You're the flash of light on a burial shroud.

G
I know something's wrong.

Am   Dadd $\frac{4}{9}$
Well, ev'ryone I know has got a rea - son

C   N.C.
To say ____ put the past away.

Chorus 2   *Repeat Chorus 1*

Verse 2

Am
Well, he's on the table and he's gone to code

C   G
And I do not think anyone knows what they are doing here.

Am
And your friends have left you, you've been dismissed.

C
I never thought it would come to this and I,

G
I want you to know

Am   Dadd $\frac{4}{9}$
Ev'ryone's got to face down the de - mons.

C   N.C.
Maybe today, ____ you could put the past away.

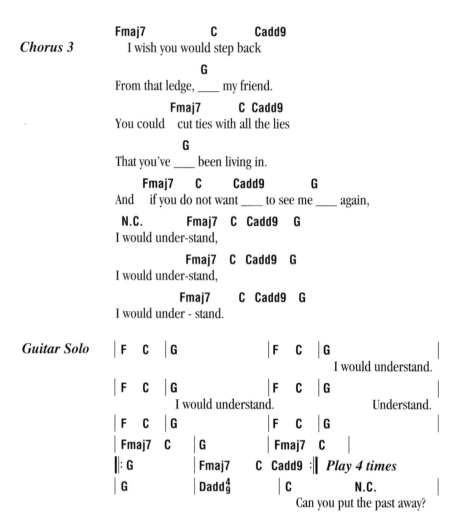

Chorus 3

Fmaj7   C   Cadd9
I wish you would step back

                G
From that ledge, ___ my friend.

         Fmaj7   C Cadd9
You could   cut ties with all the lies

         G
That you've ___ been living in.

       Fmaj7   C   Cadd9   G
And   if you do not want ___ to see me ___ again,

  N.C.   Fmaj7 C Cadd9 G
I would under-stand,

         Fmaj7 C Cadd9 G
I would under-stand,

         Fmaj7   C Cadd9 G
I would under - stand.

Guitar Solo

| F   C | G | F   C | G |

                                     I would understand.

| F   C | G | F   C | G |

          I would understand.   Understand.

| F   C | G | F   C | G |

| Fmaj7 C | G | Fmaj7 C | |

‖: G | Fmaj7   C Cadd9 :‖ *Play 4 times*

| G | Dadd$^4_9$ | C   N.C. |

                               Can you put the past away?

| | Fmaj7   C   Cadd9 |
| *Chorus 4* | I wish you would step back |

                              G
From that ledge, ____ my friend.
                        Fmaj7
I would understand.
                  C   Cadd9   G
(I wish you would step back ____ from that ledge, ____ my friend.)
                        Fmaj7
I would understand.
                  C   Cadd9   G
(I wish you would step back ____ from that ledge, ____ my friend.)
                        Fmaj7
And I would under-stand.
                  C   Cadd9   G
(I wish you would step back ____ from that ledge, ____ my friend.)
                  Fmaj7
I would under-stand.
                  C   Cadd9   G
(I wish you would step back ____ from that ledge, ____ my friend.)
                        Fmaj7   C Cadd9   G
And I would under - stand.

Outro   ‖:Fmaj7   C |G   :‖ *Play 4 times*

Knockin' on Heaven's Door

Words and Music by Bob Dylan

Ma,   take this badge off of   me.

Am   G   D/F#   D

Intro

N.C.		Am	
G D/F#	Am	
G D/F#	Am	

Verse 1

G   D/F#   Am
Ma,   take this badge off of me.

G   D/F#   Am
I can't use it anymore.

G   D/F#   Am
It's gettin' dark, too dark to see.

G   D/F#   Am
I feel like I'm knockin' on heaven's door.

Chorus 1

G   D   Am
Knock, knock, knockin' on heaven's door.

G   D   Am
Knock, knock, knockin' on heaven's door.

G   D   Am
Knock, knock, knockin' on heaven's door.

G   D   Am
Knock, knock, knockin' on heaven's door.

Verse 2

G   D/F♯   Am
Ma,   take these guns away from me.

G   D/F♯   Am
I can't shoot them anymore.

G   D/F♯   Am
There's a long, ___ black cloud followin' me.

G   D/F♯   Am
Feel like I'm knockin' on heaven's door.

Knock, knock, knock.

Chorus 2

G   D   Am
Knock, knock, knockin' on heaven's door.

G   D   Am
Knock, knock, knockin' on heaven's door.

Guitar Solo

‖: G   D/F♯ | Am | :‖ ***Play 6 times***

Verse 3

G   D/F♯   Am
Ma,   take this badge off of me.

G   D/F♯   Am
I can't use it anymore.

G   D/F♯   Am
It's gettin' dark, too dark to see.

G   D/F♯   Am
I feel like I'm knockin' on heaven's door.

Chorus 3   *Repeat Chorus 1*

Outro

‖: G   D/F♯ | Am   :‖ ***Play 4 times***
Oh, oh, oh, oh.

| G

Layla

Words and Music by
Eric Clapton and Jim Gordon

Melody:

What _ will you do when you get lone - ly? _____

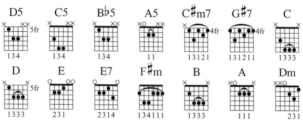

D5 C5 Bb5 A5 C#m7 G#7 C
D E E7 F#m B A Dm

Intro

‖: D5 C5 Bb5 | C5 D5 :‖ *Play 5 times*
| C5 Bb5 | C5 A5 C5 |

Verse 1

C#m7   G#7
What will you do when you get lone - ly?

C#m7   C   D   E   E7
No one waiting by your __ side.

F#m   B   E   A
You've been runnin', hidin' much too long.

F#m   B   E
You know it's just your foolish pride.

Chorus 1

A   D5 C5 Bb5
Layla,

C5   D5
Got me on my knees.

        C5 Bb5
Layla,

C5   D5
Beggin' dar-lin', please.

        C5 Bb5
Layla,

C5   D5   C5 Bb5   C5 A5 C5
Darlin', won't you ease my worried mind?

Verse 2

C#m7   G#7
Tried to give you conso-lation,

C#m7   C   D   E   E7
Your old man had let you down.

F#m   B   E   A
Like a fool, I fell in love with you.

F#m   B   E
You turned my whole world upside down.

Chorus 2

A   D5   C5 B♭5
Layla,

C5   D5
Got me on my knees.

         C5 B♭5
Layla,

C5   D5
Beggin' dar-lin', please.

       C5 B♭5
Layla,

C5   D5   C5 B♭5   C5   A5 C5
Darlin', won't you ease my worried mind?

Verse 3

C#m7   G#7
Make the best of the situ-ation,

C#m7   C   D   E   E7
Before I fin'ly go in-sane.

F#m   B   E   A
Please don't say we'll never find a way.

F#m   B   E
Tell me all my love's in vain.

Chorus 3

A   D5   C5 Bb5
Layla,

C5   D5
Got me on my knees.

        C5 Bb5
Layla,

C5   D5
Beggin' dar-lin', please.

        C5 Bb5
Layla,

C5   D5   C5 Bb5   C5   D5
Darlin', won't you ease my worried mind?

	D5 **C5 B♭5**
Chorus 4	Layla,

D5 **C5 B♭5**

Chorus 4 Layla,

C5   **D5**
Got me on my knees.

　　　C5 B♭5
Layla,

C5   **D5**
Beggin' dar-lin', please.

　　　C5 B♭5
Layla,

C5   **D5**   **C5 B♭5**   **C5**   **D5**
Darlin', won't you ease my worried mind?

Guitar Solo   ‖: **D5** **C5**   **B♭5**   │ **C5**   **D5**   :‖ *Play 8 times*

Chorus 5   *Repeat Chorus 4*

D5 **C5 B♭5**

Chorus 6 Layla,

C5   **D5**
Got me on my knees.

　　　C5 B♭5
Layla,

C5   **D5**
Beggin' dar-lin', please.

　　　C5 B♭5
Layla,

C   **Dm**
Darlin', won't you ease my worried mind?

Learning to Fly

Words and Music by
Jeff Lynne and Tom Petty

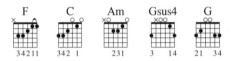

F	C	Am	Gsus4	G

Intro   ‖: F   C | Am   Gsus4   :‖   *Play 4 times*

Verse 1
             F   C   Am   Gsus4
Well, I started out

              F   C   Am   Gsus4
Down a dirty road,

F   C   Am   Gsus4
Started out

F   C   Am   Gsus4
All a-lone.

Verse 2
             F   C   Am   Gsus4
And the sun went down

           F   C   Am   Gsus4
As I crossed the hill

            F   C   Am   Gsus4
And the town lit up,

         F   C   Am   Gsus4
The world got still.

GUITAR CHORD SONGBOOK

Chorus 1

        F   C   Am   G
I'm learning to fly,

        F   C   Am   G
But I ain't got wings.

F   C   Am   G
Comin' down

      F   C   Am   G
Is the hardest thing.

Verse 3

        F   C   Am   Gsus4
Well, the good old days

     F   C   Am   Gsus4
May not re-turn,

       F   C   Am   Gsus4
And the rocks might melt,

       F   C   Am   Gsus4
And the sea may burn.

Chorus 2   **Repeat Chorus 1**

Solo   ‖: F   C | Am   G   :‖   *Play 4 times*

Verse 4

      F   C   Am   Gsus4
Well, some say life

     F   C   Am   Gsus4
Will beat you down,

     F   C   Am   Gsus4
An' break your heart,

     F   C   Am   Gsus4
And steal your crown.

Verse 5   F   C   Am   Gsus4
So I started out

     F   C   Am   Gsus4
For God knows where,

```
         F      C     Am    Gsus4
      I guess I'll know

             F    C    Am    Gsus4
      When I get there.


                 F        C   Am   G
Chorus 3    I'm learning to fly
                 F        C     Am   G
            A-round the clouds.
            F         C   Am   G
            What goes up
            F         C   Am   G
            Must come down.


Interlude   ‖: F    C    │ Am      G        :‖


                 F        C
Chorus 4    ‖: I'm learning to fly,
            Am         G
            (Learning to fly.)
                 F    C    Am   G
            But I ain't got wings.
            F    C    Am   G
            Coming down
                 F    C    Am   G
            Is the hardest thing.
                 F        C
            I'm learning to fly
            Am         G
            (Learning to fly.)
                 F    C    Am   G
            A-round the clouds.
                 F    C    Am   G
            An' what goes up
            F         C   Am   G
            Must come down.            :‖   Repeat and fade
```

Maggie May

Words and Music by
Rod Stewart and Martin Quittenton

Melody:

Wake up,   Mag - gie,   I _____

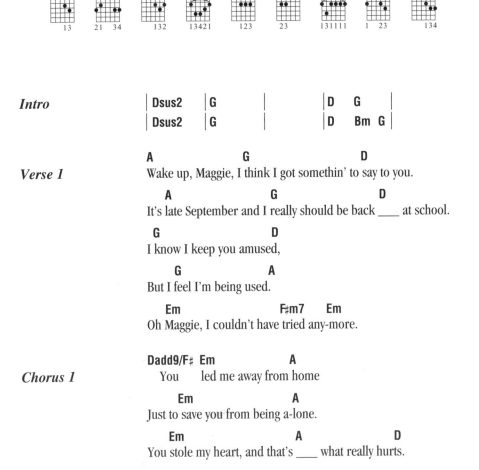

Intro

| Dsus2 | G | | | D | G | |
| Dsus2 | G | | | D | Bm G |

Verse 1

   A   **G**   **D**
Wake up, Maggie, I think I got somethin' to say to you.

   A   **G**   **D**
It's late September and I really should be back ___ at school.

G   **D**
I know I keep you amused,

      G   **A**
But I feel I'm being used.

    Em   **F#m7**   **Em**
Oh Maggie, I couldn't have tried any-more.

Chorus 1

Dadd9/F# **Em**   **A**
  You   led me away from home

    Em   **A**
Just to save you from being a-lone.

    Em   **A**   **D**
You stole my heart, and that's ___ what really hurts.

    A   **G**   **D**
The mornin' sun, when it's in your face, really shows your age.

    A   **G**   **D**
But that don't worry me none; ____ in my eyes you're ev - 'rything.

G   **D**
I laughed at all of your jokes.

     G   **A**
My love ____ you didn't need to coax.

  Em   **F♯m7** **Em** **Dadd9/F♯**
Oh Maggie, I couldn't have tried any-more.

Chorus 2

   Em   **A**
You led me away from home

     Em   **A**
Just to save you from being a-lone.

   Em   **A**   **D**
You stole my soul, and that's a pain I can do without.

Verse 3

A   **G**   **D**
All I needed was a friend to lend a guiding hand.

     A   **G**
But you turned into a lover, and mother what a lover;

       D
You wore ____ me out.

   G   **D**
All ____ you did was wreck my bed,

     G   **A**
And in the mornin' kick me in the head.

  Em   **F♯m7** **Em** **Dadd9/F♯**
Oh Maggie, I couldn't have tried any-more.

Chorus 3

   Em   **A**
You led me away from home

     Em   **A**
'Cause you didn't wanna be a-lone.

   Em   **A**   **D**
You stole my heart; I couldn't leave you if I tried.

Guitar Solo 1 | Em | A | D | G |
| Em D | G | D | |

Verse 4

    A   G   D
I suppose I could col-lect my books and get on back to school.

     A   G   D
Or steal my daddy's cue ___ and make a living out of playing pool,

    G   D
Or find myself a rock and roll band

    G   A
That needs a helping hand.

    Em   F♯m7   Em   Dadd9/F♯
Oh Maggie, I wished I'd never seen your face.

Chorus 4

             Em   A
You made a first class fool out of me,

            Em   A
But I was blind as a fool can be.

       Em   A   D
You stole my heart, but I love you anyway.

Guitar Solo 2 | Em | A | D | G |
Em D	G	D	
Em	A	D	G
Em	G

Mandolin Solo ‖: D | Dsus4 | G | D   :‖ *Play 5 times*

Outro

    D   Dsus4   G   D
Maggie, I wished I'd nev - er seen your face.

| | Dsus4 | G | D | |

                           Dsus4 G   D
I'll get on back home   one of these days.

‖: D | Dsus4 | G | D   :‖ *Repeat and fade*

Like a Rolling Stone

Words and Music by Bob Dylan

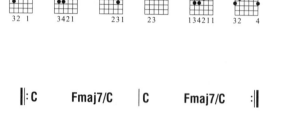

Intro ‖: C   Fmaj7/C | C   Fmaj7/C :‖

Verse 1

    C   Dm
Once upon a time you dressed so fine,

Em   F   G
Threw the bums a dime in your prime,   didn't you?

C   Dm   Em
   People call, say, ____ "Beware, doll, you're bound to fall."

                   F   G
You thought they were all   a kiddin' you.

F   G
   You used to   laugh about

F   G
   Ev'rybody that was   hangin' out.

F   Em Dm   C
   But now you don't ____ talk so loud.

F   Em Dm   C
   Now you don't seem so proud

Dm   F   G
A-bout havin' to be scrounging for your next meal.

Chorus 1

```
                   C   F   G
How does it feel?
                   C   F   G
How does it feel
                     C   F   G
To be without a home,
                     C   F   G
Like a complete un-known,
                     C   F   G
Like a rolling stone?
|C   F  |G        |         |
```

Verse 2

```
                   C          Dm           Em
Oh, you've     gone to the finest school, al-right, Miss Lonely,
                   F                    G
But you know you only used to get     juiced in it.
                   C              Dm              Em
No-body's ever taught you how to live out on the street
                        F            G
And now you're gonna have to get     used to it.
F          G              F
   You say you never compromise     with the mystery tramp,
                     G       F      Em     Dm   C
But now you    realize    he's not selling any     alibis
              F            Em    Dm      C
As you stare into the vacuum of his eyes
              Dm              F           G
And say, "Do you want to     make a deal?"
```

Chorus 2

        C **F** **G**
How does it feel?

        C **F** **G**
How does it feel

        C **F** **G**
To be on your own,

        C **F** **G**
With no direction home,

        C **F** **G**
A complete unknown,

        C **F** **G**
Like a rolling stone?

| **C** **F** | **G** | | |

Verse 3

    C   **Dm**
Oh, you   never turned a-round to see the frowns

Em   **F**   **G**
On the jugglers and the clowns when they all did   tricks for you.

C   **Dm**
Never understood that it ain't no good,

    Em   **F**   **G**
You shouldn't let other people get your   kicks for you.

F   **G**
You used to ride on a chrome horse with your   diplomat

F   **G**
Who carried on his shoulder a   Siamese cat.

F   **Em**   **Dm**   **C**
Ain't it hard ____ when you dis-cover that

F   **Em** **Dm**   **C**
He really wasn't where it's at

Dm   **F**   **G**
After he took from you ev'rything   he could steal?

Chorus 3

         C   F   G
How does it feel?

         C   F   G
How does it feel

           C   F   G
To be on your own,

               C   F   G
With no direction home,

               C   F   G
Like a complete unknown,

            C   F   G
Like a rolling stone?

| C   F | G | |

Verse 4

C   Dm   Em
  Princess on the steeple and all the pretty people,

      F   G
They're all drinkin', thinkin' that they got it made.

C   Dm
  Exchanging all precious gifts,

Em   F   G
  But you better take your diamond ring,

  You'd better pawn it, babe.

F   G
  You used to be so amused

F   G
  At Napoleon in rags and the language that he used.

F   Em   Dm   C
  Go to him now, he calls you, you can't ___ refuse.

F   Em   Dm   C
  When you ain't got nothin', ___ you got nothin' to lose.

Dm   F   G
  You're invisible now, you got no secrets to con-ceal.

Chorus 4   *Repeat Chorus 3*

Outro ||: C   F | G   :|| *Repeat and fade*

Lover, You Should've Come Over

Words and Music by Jeff Buckley

Melody:

Look-ing out the door, I see the rain

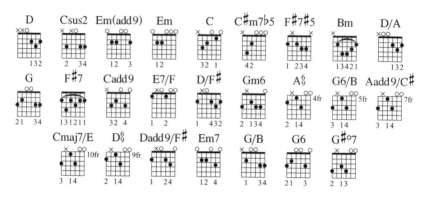

Intro

| D | | Csus2 | Em(add9) | Em | |

D
Verse 1
Looking out the door, I see the rain

　　　　　　　　　　　　Csus2　　**Em(add9)**　**Em**
Fall upon the fun'ral _____ mourners.

D　　　　　　　　　　　　　**C**
Pa-rading in a wake of sad re-lations

　　　　　　　　　　　　　Em(add9)　**Em**
As their shoes fill up with water.

　　C#m7♭5　　　　　**F#7#5**
Pre-Chorus 1　Maybe I'm too young

　　Bm　　　　　**D/A**　　**G**
To keep good love from goin' wrong.

　　D　　　　　　　　　**Csus2**
But to-night you're on my mind,

Em(add9)　　　　**Em**
So ___ you'll never know.

Verse 2

      D
Broken down and hungry for your love,

   Csus2 Em(add9)   Em
With no way to ___ feed it.

     D   **C**
Where ___ are you to-night?

              Em(add9)   **Em**
Child, you know how much I need it.

Pre-Chorus 2

  C♯m7♭5   **F♯7♯5**
Too young to hold on,

  Bm   **D/A**   **G** **F♯7**
And too old to just break free and run.

Chorus

  Bm   **Em(add9)**
Well, sometimes a man gets carried away

    Bm   **Em(add9)**
When he feels like he should be havin' his fun,

       Bm   **Em(add9)**
And much too blind to see the damage he's done.

   Cadd9   **C**
And sometimes a man must awake

               Em   **E7/F**
To find that, really, he has   no one.

D/F♯   **Gm6**
So I'll wait for you,   and I'll burn.

A⁶₉   **G6/B**
Will I ever see your ___ sweet return?

Aadd9/C♯
Oh, will I ever learn?

Cmaj7/E D⁶₉ Aadd9/C♯ G6/B
Oh, _____ lover

  A⁶₉   **Dadd9/F♯ D/F♯ Em**   **Em(add9)**
You ___ should've come   o - ver

           D
'Cause it's not too late.

Csus2 Em(add9) Em Em7 G/B
Mm.

Verse 3

   D
Lonely is the room, the bed is made,

      Csus2 Em(add9) Em
The open window lets the ____ rain in.

   D
Burn - ing in the corner is the

C   **Em(add9)**   **Em**
Only one who dreams he had you ____ with him.

Pre-Chorus 3

C♯m7♭5   **F♯7♯5**
 My body turns ____ and yearns

  Bm   **D/A** **G6**
For a, a sleep that won't ever come.

Verse 4

G♯°7 **D/A**
It's never o - ver,

       Csus2 Em(add9) **Em** **Em7**
My kingdom for a kiss up-on her ____ shoulder.

    D/A
Oh, it's never o - ver, all my riches for her smiles

     Csus2 Em(add9) Em
When I slept so soft a - gainst her.

    D/A
It's never o - ver,

      Csus2 Em(add9) Em
All my blood for the sweetness of her ____ laughter.

    D/A
It's never o - ver,

       Csus2 Em(add9) Em
She's a tear that hangs inside my soul for - ever.

C♯m7♭5   **F♯7♯5**
 Ah, but maybe I'm just too young

   Bm   **D/A** **G** **Gm6**
To keep ____ good love from ____ goin' wrong.

Outro-Chorus

D/F♯   Gm6
    Oh,   oh,

A♭⁶₉ G6/B Aadd9/C♯   Cmaj7/E D♭⁶₉
Oh,   oh, _____ oh.

Aadd9/C♯ G6/B A♭⁶₉   Dadd9/F♯ D/F♯ Em   Em(add9)
Lover,   you should have come   o - ver.

Yeah, yeah. Well yes, I,

D/F♯   Gm6
   I feel too young to hold on,

       A♭⁶₉   G6/B
And I'm much too old to break free and run.

       Aadd9/C♯   Cmaj7/E
Too deaf, dumb, and blind to see the damage I've ___ done.

D♭⁶₉   Aadd9/C♯ G6/B   A♭⁶₉
  Sweet lover, _____ you,

            Dadd9/F♯ D/F♯ Em Em(add9)
You should've come   o - ver.

Oh love, well, I'm waiting for you.

D/F♯   Gm6
  Lover, lov - er, love,

     A♭⁶₉
Lover, ___ love, love, love, love,

G6/B   Aadd9/C♯ Cmaj7/E D♭⁶₉ Aadd9/C♯   G6/B
Love, love, lov - er, lov .   -   er,

    A♭⁶₉   Dadd9/F♯ D/F# Em Em(add9)
You ___ should've come   o - ver

                D   Csus2 Em(add9)
'Cause it's not too late.

The Magic Bus

Words and Music by Peter Townshend

Melody:

Ev - 'ry day ___ I get in the queue ___

Tune down 1/2 step:
(low to high) Eb–Ab–Db–Gb–Bb–Eb

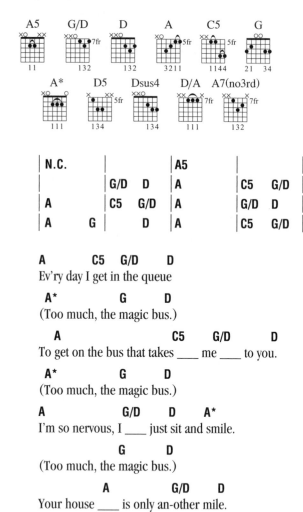

A5   G/D   D   A   C5   G

A*   D5   Dsus4   D/A   A7(no3rd)

Intro

N.C.			A5		
	G/D D	A		C5 G/D
A	C5 G/D	A		G/D D
A G	D	A		C5 G/D

Verse 1

    A   C5 G/D   D
Ev'ry day I get in the queue

A*   G   D
(Too much, the magic bus.)

    A   C5   G/D   D
To get on the bus that takes ___ me ___ to you.

A*   G   D
(Too much, the magic bus.)

A   G/D   D   A*
I'm so nervous, I ___ just sit and smile.

             G   D
(Too much, the magic bus.)

         A   G/D   D
Your house ___ is only an-other mile.

A*   G   D
(Too much, the magic bus.)

GUITAR CHORD SONGBOOK

Verse 2

A   C5   G/D D
Thank you, driver, for getting me here.

A*   G   D
(Too much, the magic bus.)

       A   C5   G/D D
You'll be an inspector, have ___ no___ fear.

A*   G   D
(Too much, the magic bus.)

A   G/D   D
I don't wanna cause ___ no fuss,

A*   G   D
(Too much, the magic bus.)

     A   G/D   D
But can I buy your magic bus?

A*   G   D
(Too much, the magic bus.)

Interlude

A5		N.C		
A5				D5
A		A*	C5	G/D

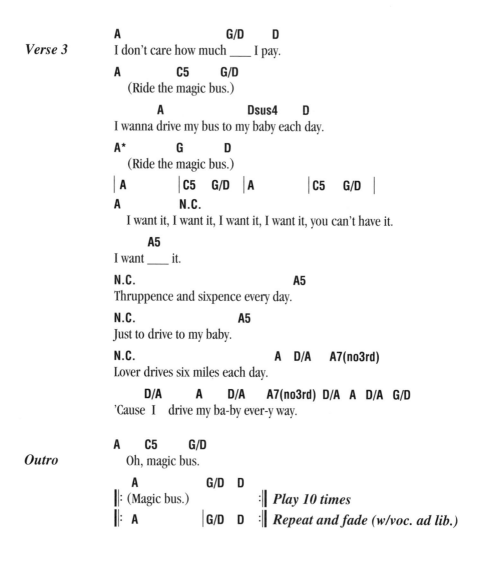

Verse 3

| A | | G/D | D |
I don't care how much ___ I pay.

| A | C5 | G/D |
(Ride the magic bus.)

| | A | | Dsus4 | D |
I wanna drive my bus to my baby each day.

| A* | G | D |
(Ride the magic bus.)

| A | | C5 | G/D | A | | C5 | G/D | |

| A | N.C. |
I want it, I want it, I want it, I want it, you can't have it.

| A5 |
I want ___ it.

| N.C. | | A5 |
Thruppence and sixpence every day.

| N.C. | A5 |
Just to drive to my baby.

| N.C. | | A | D/A | A7(no3rd) |
Lover drives six miles each day.

| D/A | A | D/A | A7(no3rd) | D/A | A | D/A | G/D |
'Cause I drive my ba-by ever-y way.

Outro

| A | C5 | G/D |
Oh, magic bus.

| A | | G/D | D |
‖: (Magic bus.) :‖ *Play 10 times*

‖: A | G/D | D :‖ *Repeat and fade (w/voc. ad lib.)*

The Man Who Sold the World

Words and Music by David Bowie

Tune down 1/2 step:
(low to high) E♭–A♭–D♭–G♭–B♭–E♭

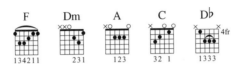

Intro

| N.C. | | | |
| F | | Dm | |

Verse 1

                A
We passed upon the stairs,
                Dm
We spoke in walls and web.
             A
Although I wasn't there,
             F
He said I was his friend,
             C
Which came as a surprise.
       A
I spoke into his eyes.
           Dm
I thought you died a long,
        C
A long, long time ago.

Chorus 1

        C   F
Oh no, __ not me,

     D♭   F
We never lost control.

          C   F
The face ____ to face

     D♭
Of a man who sold the world.

Interlude 1

| A | | | Dm | | | |
| F | | | Dm | | N.C. | |

Verse 2

                     A
I laughed and shook his hand

                        Dm
And made my way back home.

               A
I searched afar the land,

                      F
For years and years I roamed.

             C
I gazed a gazy stare.

               A
We walked a million hills.

            Dm
I must have died a long,

               C
A long, long time ago.

	C **F**
Chorus 2	Who knows? Not me.

      D♭   **F**
I never lost control.

          C   **F**
You're face ____ to face

          D♭
With the man who sold the world.

| **A** | | **Dm** | |

          C   **F**
Chorus 3   Who knows? ____ Not me.

      D♭   **F**
We never lost control.

          C   **F**
You're face ____ to face

          D♭
With the man who sold the world.

Interlude 2

| **A** | | **Dm** | |
| **F** | | | |

Guitar Solo

Dm		**A**	
Dm		**F**	
Dm		**A**	
Dm		**F**	
Dm		**A**	
Dm		**F**	

Me and Julio Down by the School Yard

Words and Music by Paul Simon

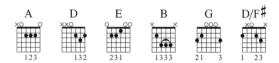

Intro ‖: A   D   A | E :‖ *Play 7 times*

Verse 1

      A
The mama pajama rolled out of bed,

          D
And she ran to the police station.

      E
When the papa found out, he began to shout,

           A   **N.C.**
And he started the investi-gation.

      E   **A**
It's against the law, it was against the law.

      E   **A**
What the mama saw, it was against the law.

Verse 2

    A
The mama looked down and spit on the ground

          D
Ev'ry time my name gets mentioned.

    E
The papa said, "Oy, if I get that boy

               A   **N.C.**
I'm gonna stick him in the house of de-tention."

Chorus 1

         D
Well, I'm on my way,

    A
I don't know where I'm goin'.

    D
I'm on my way,

      A   **B**   **E**
I'm takin' my time but I don't know where.

    D   **G**   **A**
Goodbye to Rosie, the Queen of Co-rona.

     G   **D/F#**   **E**   **A**   **D**   **A**   **E**
See you, me and Julio down by the school yard.

     A   **G**   **D/F#**   **E**   **A**   **D**   **A**   **E**
See you, me and Julio down by the school yard.

Interlude

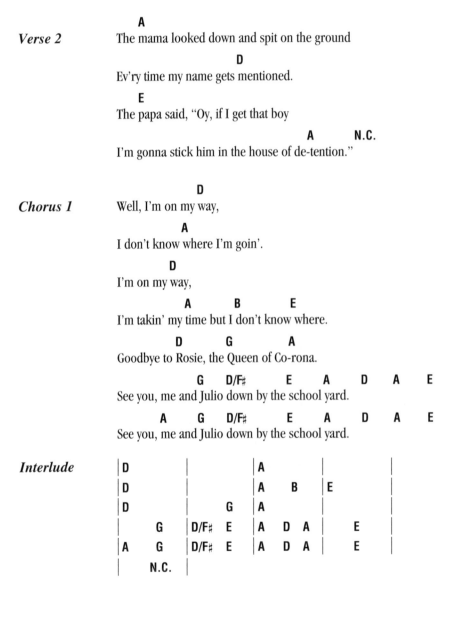

ACOUSTIC ROCK

Verse 3

A
Whoa, in a couple of days

They come and take me away,

D
But the press let the story leak,

E
And when the radical priest

Come to get me released,

A
We's all on the cover of Newsweek.

Chorus 2

D
And I'm on my way,

A
I don't know where I'm goin'.

D
I'm on my way,

A   B   E
I'm takin' my time but I don't know where.

D   G   A
Goodbye to Rosie, the Queen of Co-rona.

G   D/F♯   E   A   D   A   E
See you, me and Julio down by the school yard.

A   G   D/F♯   E   A   D   A   E
See you, me and Julio down by the school yard.

A   G   D/F♯   E   A   D   A   E
See you, me and Julio down by the school yard.

Outro   ‖: A   D   A | E   :‖ *Repeat and fade*

More Than Words

Melody:

Say-ing "I ___ love ___ you"

Words and Music by
Nuno Bettencourt and Gary Cherone

G   G/B   Cadd9   Am7   C   D   Dsus4   Em   D7   D/F#

G7   G7/B   Cm   Em7   Bm   D7♭9/A   Dm(add2)/F   Esus4   Csus2   Gm/B♭

Intro   ‖: G G/B Cadd9 | Am7 | C | D Dsus4 G   :‖

Verse 1
        G G/B   Cadd9
        Sayin', "I love you"

Am7   C   D Dsus4 G
Is not the words I want to hear from you.

G/B   Cadd9   Am7
It's not that I want you   not to say,

    C   D   Dsus4 Em   Am7 D7
But if you on - ly   knew how easy it would be,

    G   D/F#   Em
To show me how you feel.

Chorus 1
               Am7   D7   G7 G7/B C
More than words is all you have to do to make it real.

        Cm   G   Em
Then you wouldn't have to say that you love me,

       Am7 D7 G
'Cause I'd al - ready know.

                 D/F#   Em   Bm   C
What would you do__ if my heart was torn in two?

              G/B Am7
More than words to show you feel

ACOUSTIC ROCK

        D7   **G**
That your love for me is real.

                    D/F#   Em   Bm   C
What would you say___ if I took those words a-way?

                            G/B   Am7
Then you couldn't make things new

        D7   **G**
Just by say - in', "I love you."

            G G/B Cadd9   Am7
Interlude   La, dee, da , la, dee, da,

                C
Dee, dai, dai, da.

D   Dsus4 G   G/B Cadd9
More than   words.

                    Am7   D7
La, dee, da, dai, da.

            G G/B   Cadd9   Am7
Verse 2   Now that I've tried to   talk to you

            C   D   Dsus4   G
And make you un - der - stand,

G/B   Cadd9   Am7
    All you___ have to do is close your eyes

            C   D   Dsus4 Em
And just reach out your   hands

        Am7   D7   G   D/F# Em
And___ touch me, hold me close, don't ever let me go.

                    Am7   D7   G7   G7/B C
Chorus 2   More than words is all I ever needed you___ to show.

                Cm   G
Then you wouldn't have to say

                    Em
That you love me,

```
         Am7    D    D7b9/A    G
'Cause I'd al - read - y         know.

                              D/F#
What would you do

     Em        Bm      C
If my heart was torn in two?

                          G/B   Am7
More than words to show you  feel

        D7              G
That your love for me is real.

                          D/F#
What would you say

     Em        Bm      C
If I took those words a-way?

                          G/B    Am7
Then you couldn't make things new

        D7          G       G/B  Cadd9
Just by say - ing "I love    you."
```

Outro
```
                      Am7
‖: La, dee, da, dai, dai,

             C
Dee, dai, dai, da.

D    Dsus4  G    G/B  Cadd9
More than  words.    :‖  Play 3 times

             Am7
La, dee, da, dai, dai,

             C
Dee, dai, dai, da.

D    Dsus4  G       D/F#
More than  words.

Dm(add9)/F   Esus4
Oo, oo, oo, oo,

        Am7     D
Oo, oo,       oo.

N.C.      G      Csus2  G/B  Gm/Bb  Am7  G
More than words.
```

Mother Nature's Son

Words and Music by
John Lennon and Paul McCartney

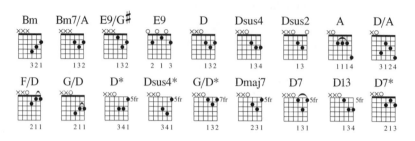

Bm Bm7/A E9/G♯ E9 D Dsus4 Dsus2 A D/A

F/D G/D D* Dsus4* G/D* Dmaj7 D7 D13 D7*

Intro

Bm Bm7/A	E9/G♯ E9
D Dsus4	Dsus2 Dsus4 D
Dsus2 D Dsus4 D	Dsus2 D Dsus2 D

Verse 1

D   Dsus4   D
Born a poor young country boy,

Bm   Bm7/A E9/G♯   E9
Mother Nature's son.

A D/A   A D/A A
All day long___ I'm sitting

D/A   A   D/A
Sing - ing songs___ for ev - 'ryone.

| D   F/D | G/D   D |
| F/D | G/D   D |

Verse 2

```
D       Dsus4           D
Sit be-side a mountain stream,

Bm      Bm7/A E9/G♯     E9
See her waters rise.

A   D/A     A D/A  A
Lis-ten  to__ the  pretty

    D/A       A    D/A       D    F/D   G/D   D
Sound__ of mu - sic as she flies.
```

Bridge 1

```
    Dsus4 D*    Dsus4* D* G/D*        D*
Do, doot,  do, do, do,     do, do, doodle, do.

        Dsus4* D* G/D*        D*    Dmaj7   D7
Do, do, do,      do,  do, doodle, do.

    D13 D7     G/D   Gm/D     D
Mm, do, ____ do.
```

Verse 3

```
D       Dsus4           D
Find me in my field of grass,

Bm      Bm7/A   E9/G♯   E9
Mother Nature's son.

A    D/A       A  D
Sway-ing  dais - ies

A       D/A  A        D/A      D   F/D   G/D   D
Sing a la - zy song beneath__ the sun.
```

	Dsus4 D*		Dsus4* D* G/D*		D*

Bridge 2

Dsus4 D*   Dsus4* D* G/D*   D*
Do, doot, do, do, do,   do, doodle, doodle, do.

Dsus4* D* G/D*   D*   Dmaj7 D7
Do, do, do,   do, do, doodle, do.

D13 D7   G/D Gm/D
Mm, do, do, do, do, do,

D   Dsus4
Yeah, yeah, yeah.

Verse 4

D Dsus4   D
Mm, mm, mm, mm, mm,

Bm Bm7/A E9/G♯ E9
Oo, oo.

A D/A A D/A   A D/A A   D/A   D F/D G/D D
Mm, _____ mm, _____ mm, __ do-wah.

F/D
Oo, ah,

G/D   D7*
Mother Nature's son.

Mrs. Robinson

Words and Music by Paul Simon

Melody:

And here's to you, ___

(Capo 2nd fret)

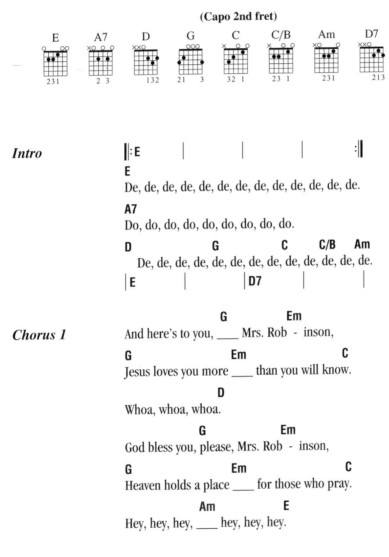

Intro

‖: E | | | :‖

E
De, de, de, de, de, de, de, de, de, de, de, de, de.

A7
Do, do, do, do, do, do, do, do, do.

D   **G**   **C**   **C/B**   **Am**
De, de, de, de, de, de, de, de, de, de, de, de, de.

| E | | D7 | | |

Chorus 1

                 G   **Em**
And here's to you, ___ Mrs. Rob - inson,

G   **Em**   **C**
Jesus loves you more ___ than you will know.

              D
Whoa, whoa, whoa.

               G   **Em**
God bless you, please, Mrs. Rob - inson,

G   **Em**   **C**
Heaven holds a place ___ for those who pray.

          Am   **E**
Hey, hey, hey, ___ hey, hey, hey.

Verse 1

      E
We'd like to know a little bit about you for our files.

      A7
We'd like to help you learn to help yourself.

D7   G   C   C/B   Am
Look around you, all ____ you see are sympa-thetic eyes.

E   D7
Stroll around the grounds un-til you feel at home.

Chorus 2   *Repeat Chorus 1*

Verse 2

      E
Hide it in a hiding place where no one ever goes.

A7
Put it in your pantry with your cupcakes.

D   G   C   C/B   Am
It's a little se - cret, just the Rob - in-son's affair.

E   D7
Most of all you've got to hide ____ it from the kids.

Chorus 3

              G   Em
Coo, coo, cachoo, ____ Mrs. Rob - inson,

G   Em   C
Jesus loves you more ____ than you will know.

               D
Whoa, whoa, whoa.

             G   Em
God bless you, please, Mrs. Rob - inson,

G   Em   C
Heaven holds a place ____ for those who pray.

          Am   E
Hey, hey, hey, ____ hey, hey, hey.

Verse 3

E
Sitting on a sofa on a Sunday afternoon,

A7
Going to the candidate's debate.

D   G
Laugh about it, shout about it,

C   C/B   Am
When you've got to choose.

E   D7
Ev'ry way you look at this you lose.

Chorus 4

               G   Em
Where have you gone, ___ Joe DiMag - gio?

G   Em   C
A nation turns its lonely eyes to you.

           D
Woo, woo, woo.

           G   Em
What's that you say, Mrs. Rob - inson,

G   Em   C
"Joltin' Joe" has left and gone away.

          Am   E
Hey, hey, hey, ___ hey, hey, hey.

Intro   ‖: E | :‖ *Repeat and fade*

My Sweet Lord

Words and Music by George Harrison

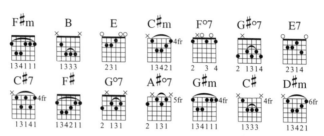

Intro

‖: F#m   B | :‖ *Play 4 times*
E C#m	E
C#m	E
F°7	G#°7
F#m   B

Verse 1

                F#m   B
My sweet Lord,

          F#m   B
Mmm, my Lord.

B   F#m   B
    Mmm, my Lord.

Chorus 1

          E   C#m
I really want to see You.

          E   C#m
Really want to be with You.

          E
Really want to see You, Lord,

      F°7   G#°7   F#m   B
But it takes so long, my Lord.

Verse 2   *Repeat Verse 1*

Chorus 2

      E   **C♯m**
I really want to know You.

      E   **C♯m**
Really want to go with You.

      E
Really want to show You, Lord,

   F°7 **G♯°7**   **F♯m** **B**
But it won't take long, my Lord.

Verse 3

       F♯m **B**
My sweet Lord.

       F♯m **B**
Mmm, my Lord.

       F♯m **B**
My sweet Lord.

Chorus 3

      E
Really want to see You.

      E7
Really want to see You.

Bridge

      C♯7
Really want to see You, Lord.

      F♯
Really want to see You, Lord,

   G°7 **A♯°7**   **G♯m** **C♯**
But it takes so long, my Lord.

Verse 4

      G♯m **C♯**
My sweet Lord.

     G♯m **C♯**
Mmm, my Lord,

     G♯m **C♯**
My, my, my Lord.

Chorus 4

              F♯   **D♯m**
I really want to know You.

        F♯   **D♯m**
Really want to go with You.

         F♯
Really want to show You, Lord,

    G°7   **A♯°7**   **G♯m**   **C♯**
And it won't take long, my ___ Lord.

       G♯m   **C♯**   **G♯m**   **C♯**
Mmm,   my sweet Lord.

      G♯m   **C♯**
My, my Lord.

Interlude

| **F♯**   **D♯m** | | **F♯**   **D♯m** | | |
| **F♯**   **G°7** | **A♯°7** | **G♯m**   **C♯** | | |

                           Mmm, my Lord.

| **G♯m**   **C♯** | **G♯m** |

          My, my, my Lord.

Verse 5

  C♯   **G♯m**   **C♯**
Oh, hmm, my sweet Lord.

    G♯m
Ooh.

Chorus 5

  C♯   **F♯**   **D♯m**
   Now I really want to see You.

          F♯   **D♯m**
I really want to be with you.

         F♯
Really want to see you, Lord,

    G°7   **A♯°7**   **G♯m**   **C♯**
But it takes so long, my___ Lord.

        G♯m   **C♯**   **G♯m**   **C♯**
My Lord,   my, my, my Lord.

        G♯m   **C♯**   **G♯m**
My sweet Lord.   My sweet Lord.

Outro

     C♯   **G♯m**
‖: My ___ Lord. :‖ *Repeat and fade*

Pinball Wizard

Words and Music by Pete Townshend

Melody:

Ev - er since I was a young _ boy,

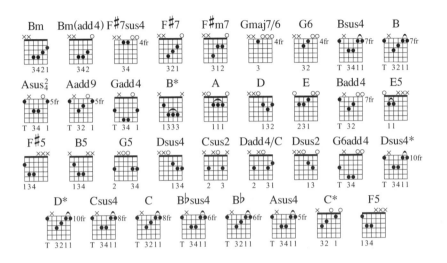

Intro

Bm	Bm(add4)	F♯7sus4	F♯7	
F♯m7	Gmaj7/6	G6	F♯7	
‖: Bsus4	B	:‖ *Play 4 times*		

Verse 1

    Bsus4   **B**
Ever since I was a young boy, I played the silver ball.

    Asus$^2_4$ **Aadd9**
From Soho down to Brighton, I must've played 'em all.

    Gadd4
But I ain't seen nothin' like him in any amusement hall.

    F♯7sus4   **N.C.**   **B*** **A** **D** **E**
That deaf, dumb and blind kid sure plays a mean pin-ball.

| **B*** | **A** **D** | **E** | |

Verse 2

Bsus4   **Badd4**

He stands like a statue, becomes part of the machine.

Asus⁴₂   **Aadd9**

Feelin' all the bumpers, always playing clean.

Gadd4   **G6**

Plays by intuition, the digit counters fall.

  F♯7sus4   **N.C.**   **B* A D E**

That deaf, dumb and blind kid sure plays a mean pin-ball.

B*	**A D**	**E**	

Chorus 1

   E5 F♯5 B5

He's a pin - ball wizard.

   E5 **F♯5 B5**

There has to be a twist.

  E5 F♯5 B5   **G5**   **D** **Dsus4** **D**

A pin - ball wizard's got such a supple wrist.

Bridge

 D   **Csus2**   **D**   **Dadd4/C**

How do you think he does ___ it? (I don't know.)

Dsus2 **Csus2 D**

What makes him so good?

Verse 3

    Bsus4   **Badd4**
Ain't got no distractions, can't hear no buzzers and bells.

      Asus$^2_4$ **Aadd9**
Don't see no lights a flashin', plays by sense of smell.

G6add4   **G6**
Always gets a replay, never seen him fall.

    F♯7sus4   **N.C.**   **B*** **A** **D** **E**
That deaf, dumb and blind kid sure plays a mean pin-ball.

| **B*** | **A** | **D** | **E** | |

Chorus 2

    E5   **F♯5 B5** **E5**   **F♯5** **B5**
I thought I   was the Bally table king

    E5 F♯5 B5   **G5**   **D** **Dsus4 D**
But I just handed my pinball crown to him.

Interlude   ‖: **Dsus4*** | **D***   :‖ *Play 4 times*

Verse 4

      Dsus4*   **D***
Even on my fav'rite table, he can beat my best.

      Csus4   **C**
His dis-ciples lead him in and he just does the rest.

     B♭sus4   **B♭**
He's got crazy flipper fingers, never seen him fall.

     Asus4   **N.C.**   **D** **C*** **F5**
That deaf, dumb and blind kid sure plays a mean pin-ball.

Outro   ‖: **B♭sus4** | :‖ *Repeat and fade*

Night Moves

Words and Music by Bob Seger

Melody:

I was a lit-tle too tall, could a used a

(Capo 1st fret)

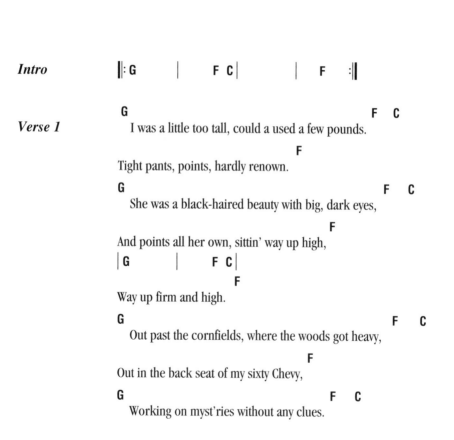

Intro   ‖: G | F C | | F :‖

Verse 1

       G   F   C
I was a little too tall, could a used a few pounds.

                           F
Tight pants, points, hardly renown.

   G   F   C
She was a black-haired beauty with big, dark eyes,

                       F
And points all her own, sittin' way up high,

 | G | F C |
                 F
Way up firm and high.

   G   F   C
Out past the cornfields, where the woods got heavy,

                     F
Out in the back seat of my sixty Chevy,

   G   F   C
Working on myst'ries without any clues.

Chorus 1

       D   **Em**   **D** **C**
Work-in' on our night moves,

       D   **Em**   **D C**
Try'n' to make some   front page, drive-in news.

       D   **Em**   **D** **C** **Cmaj7**
Work-in' on our night moves,

G   **F** **C**
In the summertime.

   F G   **F** **C**   **F**
Mm,   in the sweet summertime.

Verse 2

G   **F** **C**
We weren't in love. Oh, no, far from it.

                          F
We weren't searchin' for some pie-in-the-sky summit.

G   **F** **C**
We were just young and restless and bored,

         F
Living by the sword.

G   **F** **C**
And we'd steal away ev'ry chance we could,

                  F
To the backroom, to the alley, or the trusty woods.

G   **F** **C**
I used her, she used me, but neither one cared,

We were gettin' our share.

Chorus 2

       D   **Em**   **D** **C**
Work-in' on our night moves,

       D   **Em**   **D** **C**
Tryin' to lose the   awkward teen-age blues.

       D   **Em**   **D** **C** **Cmaj7**
Work-in' on our night moves,   mm,

G   **F**   **C**
And it was summertime.

     F **G**   **F**   **C**   **D**
Mm,   sweet summertime, sum-mertime.

Interlude 1 | **Em** | **D** |**G** |**G7** |

Bridge

     Cmaj7 **G**
And, oh, the wonder.

Cmaj7
We felt the lightning. Yeah,

F
And we waited on the thunder.

D   **G**
Waited on the thunder.

Verse 3

G
I awoke last night to the sound of thunder.

Cmaj7
"How far off?" I sat and wondered.

G
Started humming a song from nineteen-sixty-two.

Cmaj7   Em
Ain't it funny how the night moves?

C   Em
When you just don't seem to have as much to lose.

C   Em
Strange how the night moves

C Cmaj7
With autumn closing in.

Interlude 2

| G | | | | F | C |
| | | F | G | | F | C |

Mm.   Night moves.

| | | F | |

Mm.

Outro

G   F   C
||: (Night moves.) Night moves.

                F
(Night moves.) Yeah.   :|| *Play 7 times*

G
(Night moves.) Night moves.

F C   D
I remember. Oh!

Em
Ooh, ooh.

Bm
Ah, yeah, yeah, yeah, yeah.

Am   C   G
Ah,   ah.   I remember, I remember.

No Rain

By Blind Melon

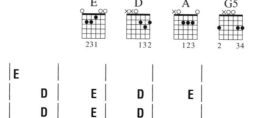

Intro
E					
	D	E	D		E
	D	E	D		

Chorus 1

E   D
All I can say is that my life is pretty plain.

A   G5   E
I like watching the puddles gather rain.

                     D
And all I can do is just pour some tea for two

     A   G5   E
And speak my point of view but it's not sane.

It's not sane.

Verse 1

     E   D   E
  I just want someone to say to me,

D
  "No, oh, oh, oh.

E   D   E   D
  I'll always be__ there when you wake."

E   D   E   D
  You know I'd like to keep my cheeks dry today.

E   D   E
So stay with me and I'll have it made.

         D
(I'll have it made.)

GUITAR CHORD SONGBOOK

Chorus 2

E   D
And I don't understand why I sleep all day

A   G5   E
And I start to complain___ that there's no rain.

D
And all I can do is read a book to stay awake,

A   G5   E
And it rips my life away___ but it's a great es-cape.

Escape, escape, escape.

Solo   ‖: E   D | :‖ *Play 8 times*

Chorus 3

E   D
All I can say is that my life is pretty plain.

A
You don't like my point of view;

G5   E
You think that I'm in-sane.

It's not sane. It's not sane.

Verse 2   **Repeat Verse 1**

Outro   D   E
         ‖: (I'll have it made.) I'll have it made.   :‖ *Play 9 times*

Norwegian Wood
(This Bird Has Flown)

Words and Music by
John Lennon and Paul McCartney

Melody:

I once had a girl, —

(Capo 2nd fret)

D   Cadd9   G/B   Dm   G   Em7   A

Intro   ‖: D | | Cadd9 G/B | D   :‖

Verse 1

D
I once had a girl,

Or should I say

Cadd9   G/B   D
She once had me?

She showed me her room,

Isn't it good,

Cadd9   G/B   D
Norwe - gian wood?

Bridge 1

Dm   **G**
She asked me to stay and she told me to sit anywhere.

Dm   **Em7   A**
So I looked around and I noticed there wasn't a chair.

Verse 2

D
I sat on a rug

Biding my time,
Cadd9   G/B D
Drinking her wine.

We talked until two,

And then she said,
Cadd9   G/B D
"It's time for   bed."

Interlude

‖: D | | Cadd9 G/B| D   :‖

Bridge 2

    Dm   G
She told me she worked in the morning and started to laugh.
    Dm   Em7   A
I told her I didn't and crawled off to sleep in the bath.

Verse 3

D
And when I awoke

I was alone,
Cadd9   G/B D
This bird had flown.

So I lit a fire,

Isn't it good,
Cadd9   G/B D
Norwe - gian wood?

Outro

|D | | Cadd9 G/B| D

Not Fade Away

Words and Music by
Charles Hardin and Norman Petty

Melody:

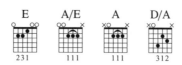

I wan-na tell ya how it's __ gon - na be.

E   A/E   A   D/A

231   111   111   312

Intro | E A/E E | A/E E | A E | A E |

Verse 1
```
            E                        A        D/A  A
            I wanna tell ya how it's gonna be.
            E                  A E        A E
            Uh, you're gonna give your love to me.
                               A        D/A  A
            I'm gonna love you night and day.
```

Chorus 1
```
            E            A E      A E
            Oh, love is love, not fade away.
                                   A    E
            Uh, well, love is love, not fade away.
```

Verse 2
```
            E                      A      D/A   A
            Uh, my love's bigger than a Cadillac.
            E                  A E        A E
            I ___try to show it and you drive me back.
                               A    D/A  A
            Uh, your love for me has got to be real,
            E            A E     A E
            For you to know just how I feel.
```

GUITAR CHORD SONGBOOK

Chorus 2

    E   A E   A E
Uh, love real, not fade away.

                     A E   A   E
Uh, well, love real, not fade away.   Yeah!

Interlude

‖:A D/A A | D/A A |E   A E | A E:‖
| A E |

Verse 3

    E   A   D/A A
I'm gonna tell ya how it's gonna be.

      E   A E   A E
Uh, you're gonna give your love to me.

                   A   D/A A
A love that lasts more than one day.

Chorus 3

        E   A E A E
Uh well, love is love, not fade away.

                A E A E
Well, love is love, not fade away.

Outro

     E   A   E   A   E
Well, love is love, not fade away.

   A   E   A   E
L-love, love, 'll not fade away.

   A   E
Not fade a-way.

   A   E
Not fade a-way.   *Fade out*

Only Wanna Be With You

Words and Music by Darius Carlos Rucker, Everett Dean Felber,
Mark William Bryan and James George Sonefeld

(Capo 2nd fret)

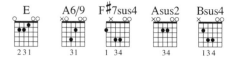

E   A6/9   F#7sus4   Asus2   Bsus4

Intro
| E   A6/9 | E   A6/9| E   A6/9| F#7sus4 |
‖: E   A6/9 :‖ *Play 4 times*

Verse 1

E   A6/9   E   A6/9
You and me, we come from diff'rent worlds,

E   A6/9   E   A6/9
You like to laugh at me when I look__ at other girls.

E   A6/9   E   A6/9
Sometimes you're crazy,   and you wonder why

E   A6/9   E   A6/9
I'm such a baby 'cause the Dol - phins make me cry.

Chorus 1

       F#7sus4
But there's nothin' I can do,

Asus2   E   A6/9   E   A6/9
I've been lookin' for a girl like you.

Verse 2

   E   **A6/9**   E   **A6/9**
You look at me, you got nothing left to say.

   E   **A6/9**   E   **A6/9**
I moan and pout at you un-til I get my__ way.

   E   **A6/9** E   **A6/9**
I won't dance,   you won't sing.

   E   **A6/9**
I just want to love you,

     E   **A6/9**
But you want to wear my__ ring.

F#7sus4

Chorus 2 But there's nothin' I can do,

Asus2   **E** **A6/9** **E** **A6/9**
I only want to be with you.

Asus2
You can call me your fool,

Bsus4   **E** **A6/9** **E** **A6/9**
I only want to be with you.

Verse 3

   E   **A6/9** E   **A6/9**
Put on a little Dylan,   sittin' on a fence.

   E   **A6/9**
I say, "That line is great."

    E   **A6/9**
You ask me what I meant by,

   E   **A6/9**
"Said I shot a man named Gray,

   E   **A6/9**
Took his wife to Italy.

   E   **A6/9**
She inherits a million bucks,

    E   **A6/9**
And when she died it came to me."

Chorus 3

      F#7sus4
I can't help it if I'm lucky,"

Asus2   **E   A6/9   E   A6/9**
   I only want to be with you.

Asus2
   Ain't Bobby so cool?

Bsus4   **E**
   I only want to be with you.

Solo   ‖: E   A6/9 | E   A6/9 :‖ *Play 8 times*

Chorus 4

      F#7sus4
Yeah, I'm tangled up in blue,

Asus2   **E   A6/9   E   A6/9**
   I only want to be with you.

      F#7sus4
You can call me your fool,

Bsus4   **E   A6/9   E   A6/9**
   I only want to be with you.

  |E   A6/9 | E   A6/9 |

Verse 4

E   A6/9 E   A6/9
Sometimes I wonder if we'll ever end.

E   A6/9
You get so mad at me

  E   A6/9
When I go out with my friends.

E   A6/9
Sometimes you're crazy,

E   A6/9
And you wonder why.

E   A6/9
I'm such a baby, yeah,

  E   A6/9
The Dol - phins make me cry.

Chorus 5

      F#7sus4
But there's nothin' I can do,

Asus2   E A6/9 E A6/9
  I only want to be with you.

    F#7sus4
You can call me your fool,

Asus2   E A6/9 E A6/9
  I only want to be with you.

    Asus2   Bsus4
Yeah, I'm tangled up in blue,

      E A6/9 E
I only want to be with you.

 A6/9   E A6/9 E
‖: I only want to be with you.   :‖ *Play 4 times*

Pink Houses

Words and Music by John Mellencamp

Melody:

Well, there's a black ___ man ___

Open G tuning:
(low to high) D–G–D–G–B–D

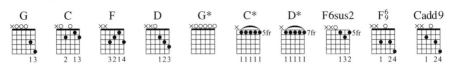

G   C   F   D   G*   C*   D*   F6sus2   F$^6_9$ Cadd9

Intro   ‖: G | C   G   :‖ *Play 4 times*

Verse 1
                                    G
Well, there's a black ___ man with a black cat,

Livin' in a black neighborhood.

He's got an interstate runnin' through his front yard,
                            F   **C**   **G**
And you know he thinks ____ he's got it so good.

And there's a woman in the kitchen,

Cleaning up the evening slop.
                    F
And he looks at her and says,"Hey darlin',
C   **G**
   I can remember when you could   stop a clock."

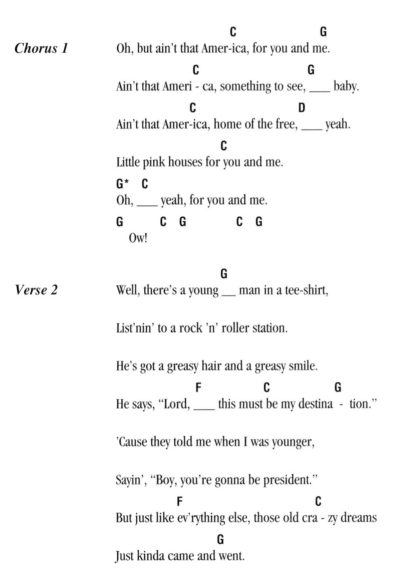

Chorus 1

                    C   G
Oh, but ain't that Amer-ica, for you and me.

               C   G
Ain't that Ameri - ca, something to see, ___ baby.

              C   D
Ain't that Amer-ica, home of the free, ___ yeah.

              C
Little pink houses for you and me.

G* C
Oh, ___ yeah, for you and me.

G   C G   C G
  Ow!

Verse 2

                           G
Well, there's a young ___ man in a tee-shirt,

List'nin' to a rock 'n' roller station.

He's got a greasy hair and a greasy smile.

                  F   C   G
He says, "Lord, ___ this must be my destina - tion."

'Cause they told me when I was younger,

Sayin', "Boy, you're gonna be president."

                F   C
But just like ev'rything else, those old cra - zy dreams

                    G
Just kinda came and went.

Chorus 2

                               C*   **G**
Oh, but ain't that Amer-ica, for you and me.

              C*   **G**
Ain't that Amer-ica, something to see, ____ baby.

              C*   **D***
Ain't that Amer-ica, home of the free, ____ yeah.

              C*
Little pink houses for you and me.

                    G   **C** **G**
Oh, build them, baby, for you and me.

| | | C   G | | | C   G | |

Interlude

‖: **F6sus2** | **C*** | **G** | | :‖ *Play 4 times*

Verse 3

                    G
Well, there's peo - ple, and more people.

What do they know, know, know?

Go to work in some high rise

          F   **C**   **G**
And va-cation down at the Gulf of Mexico, ____ ooh, yeah.

And there's winners and there's losers,

But they ain't no big deal.

                F$_9^6$ **Cadd9**
'Cause the sim - ple man, baby, pays for the thrills,

             G*
The bills, the pills that kill.

Chorus 3

         C*   G
Oh, but ain't that Amer-ica, for you and me.

     C*   G
Ain't that Amer-ica, something to see, ___ baby.

     C*   D*
Ain't that Amer-ica, home of the free, ___ yeah.

        C*
Little pink houses for you and me. Ooh.

G
 Ooh, yeah!

Chorus 4

         C*   G
Oh, but ain't that Amer-ica, for you and me.

     C*   G
Ain't that Amer-ica, something to see, ___ baby.

     C*   D*
Ain't that Amer-ica, home of the free.

           C*
Ooh, yeah, yeah, yeah, yeah, yeah, yeah, yeah.

         G
Little pink houses, babe, for you and me.

Outro

C G
Ooh, yeah.

C G   C G C G*
Ooh, yeah.

Quicksand

Words and Music by David Bowie

Melody:

I'm clos-er to the Gold - en Dawn,

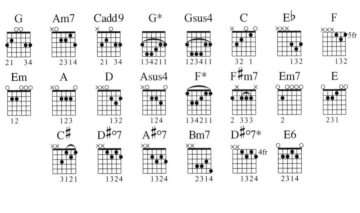

Intro ‖: G Am7 | | G Am7 | :‖

Verse 1

Cadd9
I'm closer to the Golden Dawn,

                               G*   **Gsus4 G***
Immersed in Crowley's uniform of ____ imagery.

Cadd9
I'm living in a silent film,

C   **G**
Por-traying Himmler's sacred realm of dream ____ reality.

E♭
I'm frightened by the total goal,

F
Drawing to the ragged hole,

G   **Em**   **C**
And I ain't got the power any-more.

                       G   **Am7**   **A**
No, I ain't got the power any-more.

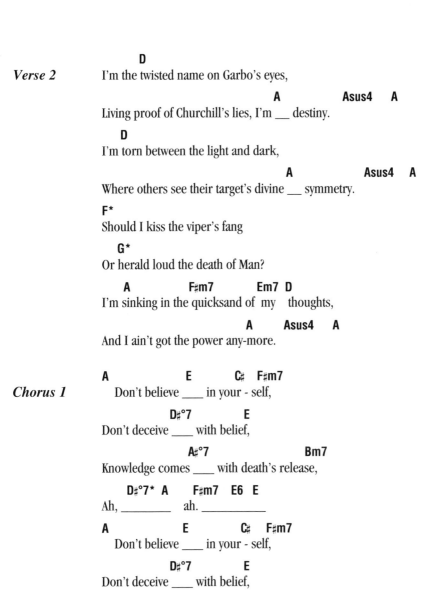

Verse 2

        D
I'm the twisted name on Garbo's eyes,

                                   A   **Asus4**   **A**
Living proof of Churchill's lies, I'm __ destiny.

        D
I'm torn between the light and dark,

                                     A   **Asus4**   **A**
Where others see their target's divine __ symmetry.

F*
Should I kiss the viper's fang

  G*
Or herald loud the death of Man?

      A   **F♯m7**   **Em7 D**
I'm sinking in the quicksand of my   thoughts,

                          A   **Asus4**   **A**
And I ain't got the power any-more.

Chorus 1

    A   **E**   **C♯** **F♯m7**
  Don't believe ___ in your - self,

          D♯°7   **E**
Don't deceive ___ with belief,

            A♯°7   **Bm7**
Knowledge comes ___ with death's release,

     D♯°7* A   **F♯m7** **E6 E**
Ah, _____ ah. _____

  A   **E**   **C♯** **F♯m7**
  Don't believe ___ in your - self,

         D♯°7   **E**
Don't deceive ___ with belief,

           A♯°7   **Bm7**
Knowledge comes ___ with death's release,

     D♯°7* A **F♯m7** **E6 E**
Ah, _____ ah. _____

Verse 3

        D
I'm not a prophet or a Stone Age man,

                                          A
Just a mortal with potential of a superman I'm __ living on.

        D
I'm tethered to the logic of homo sapien,

                                   A
Can't take my eyes from the great salvation of bullshit faith.

        F*
If I don't explain what you ought to know,

          G*
You can tell me all about it, on the next Bardot.

        A   **F♯m7**   **D**
I'm sinking in the quicksand of my   thoughts,

                              A   **Asus4**   **A**   **Asus4**
And I ain't got the power anymore.

Chorus 2

        A   **E**   **C♯** **F♯m7**
   Don't believe ___ in your - self,

              D♯°7   **E**
Don't deceive ___ with belief,

                A♯°7   **Bm7**
Knowledge comes ___ with death's release,

        D♯°7* **A**   **F#m7** **E6** **E**
Ah, _____ ah. _____

Outro   *Repeat Chorus 2 till fade*

Road Trippin'

Words and Music by Anthony Kiedis,
Flea, John Frusciante and Chad Smith

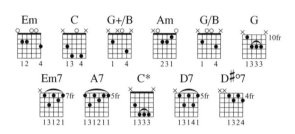

Intro   ‖: Em | |C |G+/B :‖

Verse 1

         Em   C   G+/B
         Road trippin' with my two fav'rite al-lies.

         Em   C   G+/B
         Fully loaded, we got snacks and supplies.

         Em   C   G+/B
         It's time to leave this town, it's time to steal away.

         Em   C   G+/B
         Let's go get lost any-where in the U.S.A.

         Em   C   G+/B
         Let's go get lost, let's go get lost.

Chorus 1

Em   C   G+/B
Blue, you sit so pretty west of the one.

Em   C
Sparkles light with yellow icing,

  G+/B   Em
Just a mirror for the sun.

C   G+/B   Em
Just a mirror for the sun.

C   G+/B   Am   G/B   C   G
Just a mirror for the sun.

Am   G/B   C   G
These smiling eyes ____ are just a mirror for...

Verse 2

Em   C   G+/B
So much as came before those battles lost and won.

Em   C   G+/B
This life is shining more for-ever in the sun.

Chorus 2

Em   C   G+/B
Now let us check our heads and let us check the surf.

Em   C   G   Em
Staying high and dry's more trouble than it's worth in the sun.

C   G+/B   Em
Just a mirror for the sun.

C   G+/B   Am   G/B   C   G
Just a mirror for the sun. _____

Am   G/B   C   G
These smiling eyes ____ are just a mirror for...

Interlude

‖: Em7 | A7 | C* | D7 |
| Em7 | A7 | C* | D#°7 :‖
| | | |

| | Em   C   G+/B |
| *Verse 3* | In Big Sur we take some time to linger on. |

Em   C   G+/B
We three hunky dories got our snake finger on.

Em   C   G+/B
Now let us drink the stars, it's time to steal away.

Em   C   G+/B
Let's go get lost right here in the U.S.A.

Em   C   G+/B
Let's go get lost, let's go get lost.

| | Em   C   G+/B |
| *Chorus 3* | Blue, you sit so pretty west of the one. |

Em   C
Sparkles light with yellow icing,

    G+/B   Em
Just a mirror for the sun.

C   G+/B   Em
Just a mirror for the sun.

C   G+/B   Am   G/B   C   G
Just a mirror for the sun.

Am   G/B   C   G
These smiling eyes ___ are just a mirror for...

Am   G/B   C   G
These smiling eyes ___ are just a mirror for...

Am   G/B   C   G
Your smiling eyes ___ are just a mirror for...

Outro   ‖: Em | | | :‖ *Play 3 times*

Run Around

Words and Music by John Popper

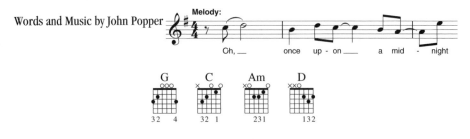

Intro   ‖: G   C   Am| D   :‖   *Play 6 times*

Verse 1

```
       G     C  Am    D
Oh, once up-on a midnight dearie
       G          C        Am   D
I woke    with some-thing in my head.
  G         C       Am   D
I couldn't es-cape the memo-ry
            G          C      Am        D
Of a phone__ call and of__ what you said.
     G          C            Am       D
Like a game show contestant with a parting gift,
            G  C      Am    D
I could not    be-lieve my eyes
            G          C        Am   D
When I saw    through the voice of a trusted friend
              G        C    Am    D
Who needs to humor me and tell me lies.
        G        C     Am     D
Yeah, hu - mor me and tell me lies.
     G    C        Am     D
And I'll lie    too, and say I don't mind,
```

```
         G        C   Am    D
And as we seek,___ so shall we find.

         G              C        Am    D
And when you're feel-ing open I'll still be here,

         G        C          Am    D
But not without a certain de-gree of fear

         G    C  Am              D
Of what will be with you and me.

             G    C        Am     D
I still    can see things hopeful-ly.
```

```
                 G  C   Am
Chorus 1    But you,

            D            G       C   Am
            Why you wanna give me a runa-round?

            D        G   C     Am          D
            Is it a sure - fire___ way to speed things up?

                 G       C      Am  D    G   C   Am   D
            When all it does is slow_____me down.
```

```
                 G    C        Am  D
Verse 2     And shake me and my confi-dence

                 G    C          Am   D
            About a great many things,

                 G       C    Am  D
            But I've been___ there, I can see it cower

                 G                 C          Am    D
            Like a nervous magician waiting in the wings

                 G  C        Am       D
            Of a bad play where the heroes are right
```

G   C   Am   D
And nobody thinks or ex-pects too much.

G   C   Am   D
And Hollywood's calling for the movie rights,

G   C   Am   D
Singing, "Hey, babe, let's keep in touch."

G   C   Am   D
Hey, ba-by, let's keep in touch."

G   C   Am   D
But I want more than a touch, I want you to reach me

G   C   Am   D
And show me all the things no one else can see.

G   C   Am   D
So what you feel becomes mine as well.

G   C   Am   D
And soon, if we're luck-y, we'd be un-able to tell

G   C   Am   D
What's yours and mine, the fishing's fine,

G   C   Am   D
And it does-n't have to rhyme, so don't you feed me a line.

Chorus 2   *Repeat Chorus 1*

Solo   ‖: G C   Am| D :‖ *Play 6 times*

Verse 3

             G   **C**
Tra, la, la bom - ba, dear,

   Am   **D**
This is the pilot speaking,

        G   **C**   **Am**   **D**
And I've   got some__ news for you.

        G   **C**
It seems my ship still stands

   Am   **D**
No mat-ter what you drop,

           G   **C**   **Am**   **D**
And there ain't a whole lot that you can do.

        G   **C**
Oh, sure, the banner may be torn

   Am   **D**
And the wind's gotten colder,

G   **C**   **Am**   **D**
   Perhaps I've grown a little cynical,

   G   **C**   **Am**   **D**
But I know no mat-ter what the waitress brings

        G **C**   **Am**   **D**
I shall drink__ in and always be full.

        G   **C**   **Am**   **D**
Yeah, I will__ drink it and always be full.

    G **C**   **Am** **D**
Oh, I like__ coffee and I like tea,

    G   **C**   **Am** **D**
But to be able to enter a final plea.

G   **C**   **Am**   **D**
I still got this dream that you just can't shake,

G   **C**   **Am**   **D**
I love you to the point you can no longer take.

       G C **Am**   **D**
Well, alright,__ okay, so be that way,

G   **C**   **Am**   **D**
I hope and pray that there's something left to say.

Chorus 3
　　　　　G　　C　　Am
But you,

D　　　　　　G　　　C　　Am
Why you wanna give me a runa-round?

D　　　G　C　　　Am　　　　D
Is it a sure - fire__ way to speed things up?

　　　　G　　　C　　Am　　　　D
When all it does is slow me down.

　　　G　　C　　Am
Oh, you.

D　　　　　　G　　　C　　Am
Why you wanna give me a runa-round?

D　　　G　C　　　Am　　　　D
Is it a sure - fire__ way to speed things up?

　　　　G　　　C　　Am　D　　G　　C　　Am　D
When all it does is slow_____me down.

Outro　　　‖: G　　C　　Am|　　D　　:‖　　*Repeat and fade*

Show Me the Way

Words and Music by Peter Frampton

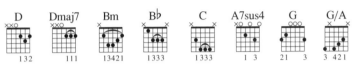

Intro ‖: D | Dmaj7 | Bm | Bb C :‖ *Play 4 times*

Verse 1

      D
I wonder how you're feeling,

         Dmaj7
There's   ringing in my ears,

      Bm
And no one to relate to

          Bb   **C**
'Cept the sea.

D
Who can I believe in?

      Dmaj7
I'm   kneeling on the floor.

      Bm
There has to be a force,

        Bb
Who do__ I phone?

Bridge 1   **A7sus4**
         The stars around me shining,

                G
         But all I really want to know...

Chorus 1   **Bm**
         Oh, won't you

                G
         Show me the way,

         Ev'ry day.

                Bm
         I want you

                G   **G/A**
         To show me the way, yeah.

Interlude 1 | **D** | **Dmaj7** | **Bm** | **Bb**   **C** |

Verse 2   **D**
         Well, I can see no reason,

                Dmaj7
         Your living on your nerves,

                Bm
         When someone drops a cup,

                Bb   **C**
         And I__ submerge.

                D
         I'm swimming in a circle,

                Dmaj7
         I   feel I'm going down.

                Bm
         There has to be a fool

                Bb
         To play__ my part.

Bridge 2   **A7sus4**
Someone thought of healing

          G
But all I really want to know...

               Bm
Chorus 2 Oh, won't you

            G
Show me the way,

Ev'ry day.

      Bm
I want you

          G
To show me the way, oh.

      Bm
I want you

    G **G/A**
Day after day,   hey.

Solo | D | | Dmaj7 | | |
         | Bm | | Bb | C |
         | D | | Dmaj7 | | |
         | Bm | | G | |

D	

Verse 3   And I wonder if I'm dreaming,

Dmaj7
I   feel so unashamed.

Bm   **Bb**
I can't believe this is happening to me.

A7sus4
Bridge 3   I watch you when you're sleeping,

                G
Oh, then I___ wanna take your love...

         Bm
Chorus 3   Oh, won't you

         G
Show me the way,

Ev'ry day.

       Bm
I want you

         G
To show me the way,

One more time.

       Bm
I want you

     G
Day after day, hey.

       Bm
I want you

     G   **G/A**
Day after day,   hey.

Interlude 2 | D | Dmaj7 | Bm | G |

                          Bm
Chorus 4   I want you

                                  G
          To show me the way

          Ev'ry day.

               Bm
          I want you

                                  G
          To show me the way

          Night and day.

               Bm
          I want you

               G   **G/A**
          Day after day,

               D
          Hey, hey,

           Dmaj7   **Bm**   **Bb C**   **D**
          Oh.

Seven Bridges Road

Words and Music by Stephen T. Young

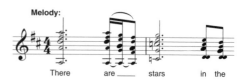

Melody:

There   are   stars   in the

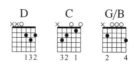

D   C   G/B

Verse 1

N.C.
There are stars in the southern sky,

Southward as you go.

There is moonlight and moss in the trees

Down the Seven Bridges Road.

Interlude

D			C	
G/B	D			

Verse 2

```
        D     C   G/B       D
Now I have loved you like a ba - by,
            C       G/B  D
Like some lonesome child.
            C   G/B       D
And I have loved you in a tame ____ way,
            C   G/B  D
And I have loved wild.
```

Bridge

```
          C                D
Some-times there's a part ____ of me
          C                D
Has to turn from here and go.
C                         D
Runnin' like a child from these warm stars
              C       G/B  D
Down the Seven Bridges Road.
```

Verse 3

```
N.C.
There are stars in the southern sky,

And if ever you decide you should go,

There is a taste of time sweet and honey

Down the Seven Bridges Road.
```

Silent Lucidity

Words and Music by Chris DeGarmo

Melody:

Hush now, don't you cry, _____

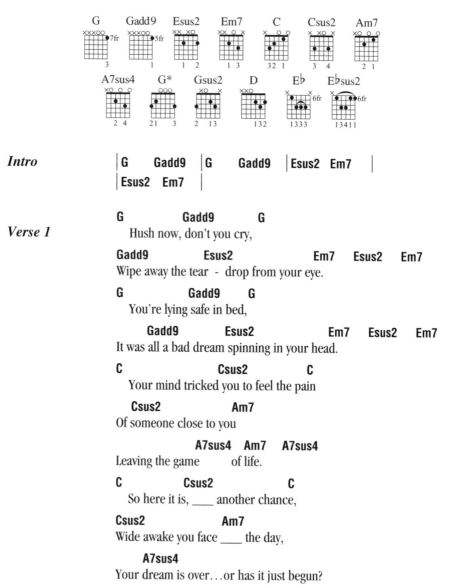

Intro

| G Gadd9 | G Gadd9 | Esus2 Em7 |
| Esus2 Em7 |

Verse 1

G   Gadd9   G
Hush now, don't you cry,

Gadd9   Esus2   Em7   Esus2   Em7
Wipe away the tear - drop from your eye.

G   Gadd9   G
You're lying safe in bed,

Gadd9   Esus2   Em7   Esus2   Em7
It was all a bad dream spinning in your head.

C   Csus2   C
Your mind tricked you to feel the pain

Csus2   Am7
Of someone close to you

A7sus4 Am7   A7sus4
Leaving the game   of life.

C   Csus2   C
So here it is, ____ another chance,

Csus2   Am7
Wide awake you face ____ the day,

A7sus4
Your dream is over…or has it just begun?

Interlude |G*   Gsus2 |G*   Gsus2 |Esus2 Em7 |
    |Esus2 Em7 |

        G*   **Gsus2**   **G***
Verse 2   There's a place I like to hide,

        Gsus2   **Esus2**   **Em7**   **Esus2**   **Em7**
        A doorway that I run through in the night.

        G*   **Gsus2**   **G**
        Relax, child, you were there,

          Gsus2 **Esus2**   **Em7**   **Esus2**   **Em7**
        But only didn't realize it, and you were scared.

        C   **Csus2**   **C**   **Csus2**
        It's a place where you will learn ____ to face your fears,

         Am7   **A7sus4**   **Am7**   **A7sus4**
        Re-trace the years and ride the whims of your mind.

        C   **Csus2**   **C**
        Commanding in another world,

        Csus2   **Am7**   **A7sus4**   **Am7**   **A7sus4**
        Suddenly, you hear and see this magic new dimen - sion.

        D   **C**
Chorus 1   (I…) _____ Will be watching over you.

        D   **C**
        (I…) _____ Am gonna help to see it through.

        D   **C**
        (I…) _____ Will protect you in the night.

        D   **Csus2**
        (I…) _____ Am smiling next to you,

              G   **Gadd9**   **G**   **Gadd9**
        In silent lucidity.

Guitar Solo |E♭   E♭sus2 |E♭   E♭sus2 |Csus2   C |
             |Csus2   C |E♭   E♭sus2 |E♭   E♭sus2 |
             |Csus2   C |N.C.(C/B♭) |N.C.(A♭) |
             |(G) |(F) |(E♭) |
             |(D) |(C) |(B♭) |
             |(A♭) |(G) |

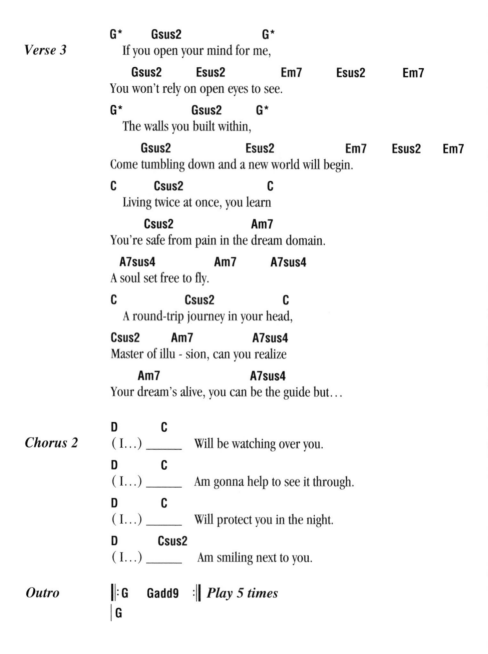

Verse 3

G*   Gsus2   G*
If you open your mind for me,

    Gsus2   Esus2   Em7   Esus2   Em7
You won't rely on open eyes to see.

G*   Gsus2   G*
The walls you built within,

    Gsus2   Esus2   Em7   Esus2 Em7
Come tumbling down and a new world will begin.

C   Csus2   C
Living twice at once, you learn

    Csus2   Am7
You're safe from pain in the dream domain.

A7sus4   Am7   A7sus4
A soul set free to fly.

C   Csus2   C
A round-trip journey in your head,

Csus2   Am7   A7sus4
Master of illu - sion, can you realize

    Am7   A7sus4
Your dream's alive, you can be the guide but...

Chorus 2

D   C
(I...) _____ Will be watching over you.

D   C
(I...) _____ Am gonna help to see it through.

D   C
(I...) _____ Will protect you in the night.

D   Csus2
(I...) _____ Am smiling next to you.

Outro   ‖: G   Gadd9 :‖ *Play 5 times*
           | G

Space Oddity

Words and Music by David Bowie

Melody:

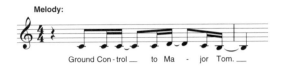

Ground Con-trol __ to Ma - jor Tom. __

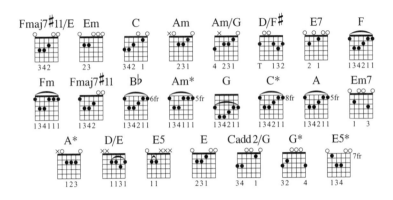

Intro   ‖: Fmaj7#11/E |Em   :‖ *Play 4 times*

Verse 1
      C   Em
      Ground Control to Major Tom.
      C   Em
      Ground Control to Major Tom.

      Am   Am/G   D/F#
      Take your protein pills and put your helmet on.

Verse 2
      C   Em
      Ground Control to Major Tom,
      C   Em
      Commencing countdown; engines on.

      Am   Am/G   D/F#
      Check ig-nition and may God's love be with you.
      |N.C. | | |

| | C   E7
| *Chorus 1* | This is Ground Control to Major Tom,
| | F
| | You've really made the grade
| | Fm   C   F
| | And the papers want to know ___ whose shirts you wear.
| | Fm   C   F
| | Now it's time to leave the capsule if you dare.
| | C   E7
| | This is Major Tom to Ground Control,
| | F
| | I'm stepping through the door
| | Fm   C   F
| | And I'm floating in a most ___ a peculiar way
| | Fm   C   F
| | And the stars ___ look very different today.

| | Fmaj7♯11 Em
| *Bridge 1* | For here am I sitting in a tin can,
| | Fmaj7♯11   Em
| | Far above the world.
| | B♭   Am*   G   F
| | Planet Earth is blue and there's nothing I can do.

Interlude 1		C* F G A	C* F G A	Fmaj7♯11
		Em7	A*	C
		D/E	E5	

Chorus 2

C   E7
Though I'm past one hundred thousand miles

                   F
I'm feeling very still

     Fm   C   F
And I think my spaceship knows which way to go.

     Fm   C   F
Tell my wife I love her very much. She knows.

G   E
Ground Control to Major Tom,

    Am   Am/G
Your circuit's dead, there's something wrong.

      D/F♯
Can you hear me, Major Tom?

      C   Cadd2/G
Can you hear me, Major Tom?

     G*
Can you hear me, Major Tom?

Can you...

Bridge 2

Fmaj7♯11   Em
Here am I   floating 'round my tin can,

Fmaj7♯11   Em
Far above the moon.

B♭   Am*   G   F
Planet Earth is blue and there's nothing I can do.

Interlude 2

C* F G A	C* F G A	Fmaj7♯11	
Em7	A*	C	
D/E			

Outro

‖: E5* | :‖ *Repeat and fade*

Somebody to Love

Words and Music by Darby Slick

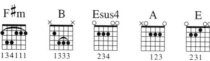

F#m   B   Esus4   A   E

134111   1333   234   123   231

Verse 1

            F#m   **B**
When the truth is found

    Esus4 F#m
To be_____ lies,

                B
And all the joy

    Esus4 F#m
With-in you_____ dies,

Chorus 1

    N.C.   **A**   **E**   **F#m**
Don't you want some-body to love?

B   **A**   **E**   **F#m**
Don't you need some-body to love?

B   **A**   **E**   **F#m**
Wouldn't you love some-body to love?

B   **A**   **B**   **F#m**
You better find__ some-body to love.

Interlude 1 | **B** | **F#m**   **E** | **F#m** | |

Verse 2

          F#m   **B**
When the garden's flowers,

    Esus4   **F#m**
Ba - by, are____ dead,

Yes, and your mind,

        B E   **F#m**
Your mind__   is so full of red.

Chorus 2   ***Repeat Chorus 1***

                F#m
Verse 3   Your eyes,

I say your eyes may look like his.

                   B
Yeah, but in your head, baby,

                F#m
I'm afraid you don't know where it is.

Chorus 3   ***Repeat Chorus 1***

Interlude 2 | E | B   A | | F#m | |

          F#m   **B**
Verse 4   Tears are running,

               F#m   **B** **E**
They're all run - ning down your breast,

          F#m   **B**
And your friends, baby,

          E   **F#m**
They treat you like a guest.

Chorus 4   ***Repeat Chorus 1***

Outro | F#m | B | | |
            | F#m | E | F#m | B   E |
            | F#m | B   E | F#m | B   E |
            | F#m | | A   E | B |
            | A   E | B | A   E | B | A   B |

Someday I'll Be Saturday Night

Words and Music by Desmond Child,
Jon Bon Jovi and Richie Sambora

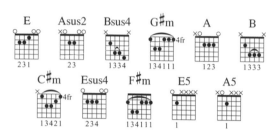

Intro

   E
Hey, man, I'm alive,

   Asus2
I'm tak - ing each day a night at a time.

   Bsus4
I'm feeling like a Monday,

           E
But someday I'll be Saturday ___ night.

Verse 1

   E
Hey, my name is Jim, where did I go wrong?

   G#m
My life's a bargain basement, all the good shit's gone.

  A
I just can't hold a job. And where do I belong?

    E   **Bsus4**   **E**
Been sleeping in my car, my dreams move on.

Verse 2

E
My name is Billy Jean, my love is bought and sold.

G♯m
I'm only sixteen; I feel a hundred years old.

A
My foster daddy went, took my innocence away.

B   **Bsus4**   **B**
The street life ain't much better but at least I'm get-ting paid.

Pre-Chorus 1

          C♯m   **A**
And Tuesday just might come ___ my way.

E   **Esus4**   **E**
It can't get worse than yes-terday.

G♯m
Thursdays, Fridays, ain't been kind.

A   **F♯m**
But somehow I've survived.

Chorus 1

E
Hey, man, I'm alive,

          A
I'm tak - ing each day a night at a time.

E   **Bsus4**
Yeah, I'm down, but I know I'll get by.

B **Bsus4**   **B**   **A**   **B**
Hey, hey,   hey, hey ___ man, gotta live my life

        E   **C♯m**
Like I ain't got nothing but this roll of the dice.

    Bsus4   **B**
I'm feeling like a Monday,

        Asus2   **E**   **A**
But some - day I'll be Saturday ___ night.

Verse 3

    E
Now, I can't say my name or tell you where I am.

    G♯m
I wanna blow myself away, don't know if I can.

   A
I wish that I could be in some other time and place.

   B   **Bsus4**   **B**
With someone else's soul, some - one else's face.

Pre-Chorus 2

   C♯m   **A**
Or Tuesday just might come ____ my way.

   E   **Esus4** **E**
It can't get worse than yes-terday.

G♯m
Thursdays, Fridays, ain't been kind.

   A   **F♯m**
But somehow I've survived.

Chorus 2

 E
Hey, man, I'm alive,

    A
I'm tak - ing each day a night at a time.

E   **Bsus4**
Yeah, I'm down, but I know I'll get by.

B **Bsus4** **B**   **A**   **B**
 Hey, hey, hey, hey ____ man, gotta live my life

    E   **C♯m**
Like I ain't got nothing but this roll of the dice.

  Bsus4   **B**
I'm feeling like a Monday,

    Asus2   **E**
But some - day I'll be Saturday ____ night.

Guitar Solo

| A | | | E | | |
| A | | | E | | E5 | |

Ooh.

| A5 | | | E | | E5 | |

Saturday night.

| A5 | | | |

Bridge

E5
Someday I'll be Saturday night.

A5
I'll be back on my feet. I'll be doing alright.

E5
It may not be tomorrow, baby; that's o.k.

A5
I ain't going down, gonna find a way. Hey, hey, hey.

Chorus 3

E
Hey, man, I'm alive,

A
I'm tak - ing each day a night at a time.

E   Bsus4
Yeah, I'm down, but I know I'll get by.

B Bsus4   B   A   B
  Hey, hey,   hey, hey ____ man, gotta live my life

E   C♯m
Like I ain't got nothing but this roll of the dice.

Bsus4   B
I'm feeling like a Monday,

Asus2   E
But some - day I'll be Saturday ____ night.

B
Oh, I'm feeling like a Monday,

A   E
But some - day I'll be Saturday night.

Outro

‖: A | | E | :‖ *Repeat and fade*
(w/voc. ad lib.)

The Sound of Silence

Words and Music by Paul Simon

Melody:

Hel-lo dark-ness, my old friend,

(Capo 4th fret)

Bsus2   A   G   D   Bm

Verse 1

    Bsus2   **A**
    Hello darkness, my old friend,

                      Bsus2
    I've come to talk with you a-gain.

                 G   **D**
    Because a vision softly ___ creeping,

                G   **D**
    Left it's seeds while I was ____ sleeping.

    G   **D**
    And the vision that was planted in my brain

        Bm D   **A**   **Bm**
    Still remains   within the sound of silence.

Verse 2

                     A
    In restless dreams I walked a-lone

                Bm
    Narrow streets of cobble-stone.

               G   **D**
    'Neath the halo of a ____ streetlamp

                G   **D**
    I turned my collar to the cold and damp.

    G   **D**
    When my eyes were stabbed by the flash of a neon light

         Bm D   **A**   **Bm**
    That split the night   and touched the sound of silence.

Verse 3

               A
And in the naked light I saw
               Bm
Ten thousand people, maybe more.
          G   **D**
People talking without ___ speaking;
          G   **D**
People hearing without ___ list'ning.
    G   **D**
People writing songs that voices never share.
      Bm **D**   **A**   **Bm**
And no one dare   disturb the sound of silence.

Verse 4

               A
"Fools!" said I, "You do not know
           Bm
Silence like a cancer grows.
          G   **D**
Hear my words that I might ___ teach you.
          G   **D**
Take my arms that I might ___ reach you."
  G   **D**
But my words like silent raindrops fell,
Bm **D**   **A**   **Bm**
And echoed in the wells of silence.

Verse 5

               A
And the people bowed and prayed
          Bm
To the neon god they made.
          G   **D**
And the sign flashed out its ___ warning.
          G   **D**
In the words that it was ___ forming.
          G
And the signs said, "The words of the prophets
              D   **Bm**
Are written on the subway walls ___ and tenement halls."
D   **A**   **Bm**
Whisper the sounds of silence.

Strong Enough

Words and Music by Kevin Gilbert,
David Baerwald, Sheryl Crow, Brian McLeod,
Bill Bottrell and David Ricketts

Melody:

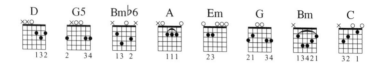

God, I feel — like hell — to - night.

Intro

‖: D   G5 |Bm♭6   A   :‖ *Play 4 times*

Verse 1

D   G5   Bm♭6   A
God, I feel like hell ___ to-night.

D   G5   Bm♭6   A
Tears of rage I can - not fight.

            D   G5   Bm♭6
I'll be the last to help you un - der-stand.

A   D   G5   Bm♭6
Are you strong enough to be ___ my man?

A   D   G5   Bm♭6   A
My ___ man.

Interlude 1 ‖: D   G5 |Bm♭6   A   :‖ *Play 3 times*

Verse 2

D   G5   Bm♭6 A
Nothing's true and noth - ing's right.

D   G5   Bm♭6 A
Just let me be alone ____ to-night,

D   G5   Bm♭6
'Cause you can't change the way ____ I am.

A   D   G5   Bm♭6 A
Are you strong enough to be ____ my man?

Chorus 1

Em D   G   A
Lie ____ to me,

Bm   C   G   A
I promise, I believe.

Em D   G   A
Lie ____ to me,

Bm   C G A
But please, don't leave.

Interlude 2 | D   G5 |Bm♭6   A |
                                Don't leave.

‖: D   G5 |Bm♭6   A :‖ *Play 3 times*

Verse 3

```
              D           G5   Bm♭6   A
I have a face I can  -  not show.

   D                    G5    Bm♭6   A
I make the rules up as ____ I go.

      D               G5       Bm♭6
Just try and love me if ____ you can.

A      D                  G5      Bm♭6   A
Are you strong enough to be ____ my man?

      D    G5   Bm♭6
My ____ man.

A      D                  G5      Bm♭6
Are you strong enough to be my man?

A      D                  G5      Bm♭6
Are you strong enough to be my man?

A      D                  G5       Bm♭6      A
Are you strong enough to be ____ my man?
```

Verse 4

```
               D              G5      Bm♭6   A
Now when I show you that I just ____ don't care,

              D              G5      Bm♭6   A
When I'm throwing punches in ____ the air,

              D           G5      Bm♭6
When I'm broken down and I ____ can't stand,

      A    D              G5      Bm♭6   A
Would you be man enough to be ____ my man?
```

Chorus 2

```
Em  D      G    A
Lie ____ to me,

  Bm     C     G    A
I promise, I believe.

Em  D      G    A
Lie ____ to me,

   Bm     C    G    A
But please, don't leave.
```

Sweet Jane

Words and Music by Lou Reed

Melody:

Stand - ing on the cor - ner,

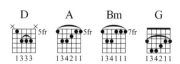

D	A	Bm	G
5fr	5fr	7fr	
1333	134211	134111	134211

Intro   ‖: D   A |Bm G   A |D   A |Bm A G A :‖

Verse 1

D A   G   Bm A D
Standing on the corner,

A   G   Bm   A   D
Suit-case in my hand.

A   G   Bm   A   D
Jack is in his corset, Jane is in her vest,

A   G Bm   A   D
And me I'm in a rock and roll band.   Huh.

A   G   Bm   A   D
Ridin' in a Stutz Bearcat, Jim,

A   G   Bm A   D
You know those were diff'rent ___ times.

A   G   Bm
Oh, all the poets, they studied rules of verse,

A   D   A   G Bm A   D
And those ___ ladies, they rolled their eyes.

Chorus 1

```
D           G   A   D
Sweet Jane, ___ whoa.
          G  A   D
Sweet Jane, ____ oh, oh.
        G    A   D
Sweet Jane.
```

Verse 2

```
D                    A   G         Bm  A  D
    I'll tell you something, Jack, he is a banker,
          A  G         Bm   A   D
And Jane, ____ she is a clerk.
          A     G       Bm   A   D
And both of them save their monies,
                A      G         Bm   A  D
Ha, and when, when they come home from work.
      A       G      Bm  A  D
Ooh, sittin' down by the fire, ___ oh,
          A   G     Bm   A    D
The radi-o does ___ play    the clas-sical music there, Jim,
        A    G           Bm
"The March of the Wooden Sol-diers."
A       D           A     G   Bm  A      D
All you pro-test kids, you can hear Jack ___ say,  get ready, ah.
```

Chorus 2   *Repeat Chorus 1*

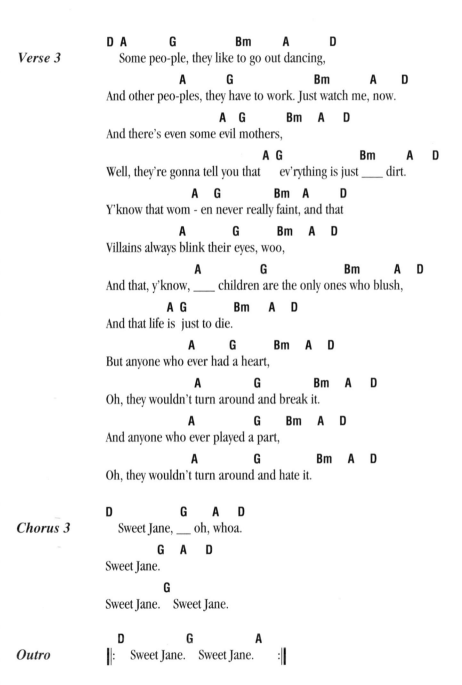

Verse 3

```
          D A    G          Bm    A    D
          Some peo-ple, they like to go out dancing,
               A    G           Bm    A    D
          And other peo-ples, they have to work. Just watch me, now.
                    A  G     Bm  A   D
          And there's even some evil mothers,
                         A G           Bm     A    D
          Well, they're gonna tell you that     ev'rything is just ___ dirt.
                    A   G      Bm  A    D
          Y'know that wom - en never really faint, and that
                    A      G     Bm  A   D
          Villains always blink their eyes, woo,
                    A        G           Bm       A   D
          And that, y'know, ___ children are the only ones who blush,
                    A G    Bm   A    D
          And that life is  just to die.
                    A     G     Bm  A   D
          But anyone who ever had a heart,
                    A        G        Bm   A    D
          Oh, they wouldn't turn around and break it.
                    A       G    Bm  A   D
          And anyone who ever played a part,
                    A        G        Bm   A   D
          Oh, they wouldn't turn around and hate it.
```

Chorus 3

```
          D         G    A   D
          Sweet Jane, __ oh, whoa.
                G    A   D
          Sweet Jane.
                    G
          Sweet Jane.   Sweet Jane.
```

Outro

```
          D         G         A
          ‖:  Sweet Jane.   Sweet Jane.    :‖
```

Suite: Judy Blue Eyes

Words and Music by Stephen Stills

Melody:

It's   get-ting   to ___ the   point ___

Open E5 tuning:
(low to high) E–E–E–E–B–E

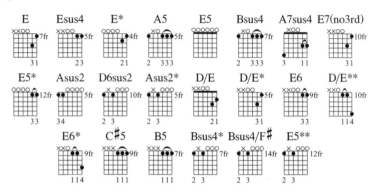

E   Esus4   E*   A5   E5   Bsus4   A7sus4   E7(no3rd)

E5*   Asus2   D6sus2   Asus2*   D/E   D/E*   E6   D/E**

E6*   C#5   B5   Bsus4*   Bsus4/F#   E5**

Intro

| E | | Esus4 | E* | | |

| E | | Esus4 | E* | |

                               A5

Verse 1   It's getting to the point

                  E5   **Bsus4**

Where I'm no fun anymore.

       A5   **A7sus4**

I am sorry.

E5   **A5**

Sometimes it hurts

         E5   **Bsus4**

So badly I must cry out loud.

     A5   **A7sus4**

I am lonely.

Chorus 1

     E5   **Bsus4**
I am yours, ___ you are mine,

     A5   **A7sus4**
You are what ___ you are.

     E5 **A5**
You make it hard.

Verse 2

    E*   **A5**
Re-member what we've said

     E5   **Bsus4**
And done and felt about each other.

      A5 **A7sus4**
Oh, babe, have mercy.

E5   **A5**
 Don't let the past

     E5   **Bsus4**
Remind us of what we are not now.

     A5 **A7sus4**
I am not dreaming.

Chorus 2

     E5   **Bsus4**
I am yours, ___ you are mine,

     A5 **A7sus4**
You are what you are.

     E5
You make it hard.

Interlude 1 | E | Esus4 | E* | |
              Oh, _____ oh, oh.
      | E E7(no3rd) | E Esus4 | E* |

Verse 3

    E*   **A5**
    Tearing yourself

       E5   **Bsus4**
    Away from me now, you are free,

      A5 **A7sus4**
    And I am crying.

    E5   **A5**
    This does not mean

        E5
    I don't love you, I do,

      Bsus4
    That's for-ever,

      A5   **A7sus4**
    Yes, and for always.

Chorus 3   *Repeat Chorus 1*

Verse 4

    E*   **A5**
    Something inside

       E5   **Bsus4**
    Is telling me that I've got your secret.

      A5   **A7sus4**
    Are you still list'ning?

    E5   **A5**
    Fear is the lock

       E5   **Bsus4**
    And laughter the key to your heart.

     A5   **A7sus4**
    And I love you.

Chorus 4

             E5   **Bsus4**
I am yours, ____ you are mine,

             A5   **A7sus4**
You are what ____ you are.

            E5   **A5**
You make it hard.

               E5   **A5**
And you make it hard.

               E5   **A5**
And you make it hard.

               E5
And you make it hard.

Interlude 2 | **E5***   **Esus4 E*** | **E5***   **Esus4 E*** |

Bridge 1

E5*   **Esus4 E***   **E5***   **Esus4 E***
  Fri -   day eve - ning,

E5*   **Esus4 E***   **Asus2**   **A7sus4**
  Sun-day in _____ the af - ternoon.

                 E5*   **Esus4 E* E5***   **Esus4 E***
What have you got to lose?

Bridge 2

E5*   **Esus4 E***   **E5* Esus4 E***
  Tues -   day morn - ing,

E5*   **Esus4 E***   **Asus2**   **A7sus4**
  Please be gone, ____ I'm tired of you.

                 E5*   **Esus4 E* E5***   **Esus4 E***
What have you got to lose?

        D6sus2
Can I tell it like it is?

        Asus2*
But listen to me, baby.

D6sus2   **Asus2***
  It's my heart that's a suff'rin', it's a dyin'.

                 E5*   **Esus4 E* E5***
That's what I have to lose.

Bridge 3

E5   Esus4 E*   E5*   Esus4 E*

I've _____ got an an - swer,

E5*   Esus4 E* Asus2   A7sus4

I'm go - ing to fly away.

                    E5* Esus4 E* E5* Esus4 E*

What have I got to lose?

Bridge 4

E5*   Esus4 E*   E5*   Esus4 E*

Will _____ you come see me

E5*   Esus4   E* Asus2   A7sus4

Thurs-days and ____ Saturdays? Hey, (hey,) hey.

                   E5* Esus4 E* E5*

What have you got to lose?

Guitar Solo 1   ‖: E5 | | | :‖ *Play 4 times*
| | |

Verse 5

D/E   E*

Chestnut brown canar - y,

D/E   Esus4 E*

Ruby throated spar   -   row,

D/E*   E   E6   E7(no3rd)

Sing a song,   don't be long,

                 D/E** E6*

Thrill me to the mar   -   row.

Guitar Solo 2   ‖: E5 | | | :‖
| |

Verse 6

D/E   E*

Voices of the an - gels,

D/E   Esus4 E*

Ring around the moon   -   light,

D/E*   E   E6   E7(no3rd)

Asking me, said she so free,

                 D/E** E6*

"How can you catch the spar   -   row?"

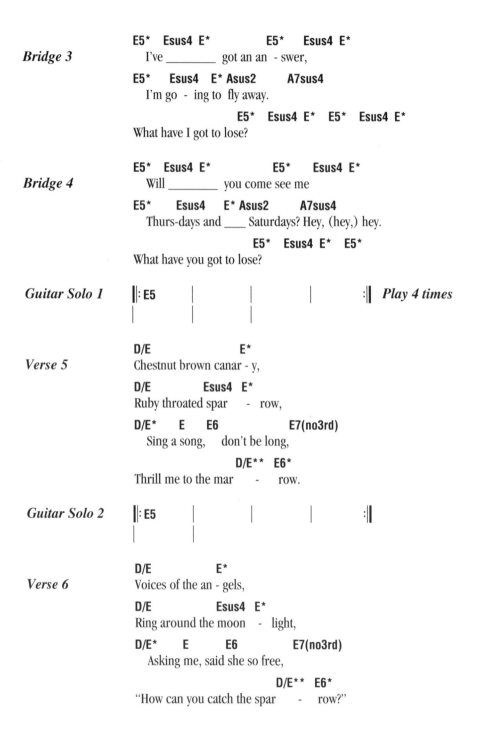

Guitar Solo 3   ‖: E5 | | | :‖

         | |

Verse 7
```
D/E              E*    Esus4  E*
Lacy, lilting lyr - ic,
D/E                    Esus4  E*
Losing love, lament    -    ing,
D/E*            E              E7(no3rd)
Change my life,    make it right,
            D/E**  E6*
Be my la    -    dy.
```

Interlude 3
```
|D/E**            |E6*          |D/E**        |E6*      |
|D/E**  E6*  D/E**|  E6*  D/E**|  E6*  C♯5  |  B5     |
```

Outro
```
        N.C.
‖: Do, do, do, do, do,

Do, do, do, do, do, do.

Do, do, do, do, do,

Do, do, do, do.  :‖
```

‖: Asus2* Bsus4* Bsus4/F♯ D6sus2   E5** :‖ *Play 8 times*

```
Asus2*    Bsus4*  Bsus4/F♯ D6sus2    E5**
Do, do, do, do, do,   do,       do, do, do, do, do.
Asus2*    Bsus4*  Bsus4/F♯ D6sus2  E5**
Do, do, do, do, do,   do,       do,     do, do.
Asus2*    Bsus4*  Bsus4/F♯ D6sus2    E5**
Do, do, do, do, do,   do,       do, do, do, do, do.
Asus2*    Bsus4*  Bsus4/F♯ D6sus2  E
Do, do, do, do, do,   do,       do,     do, do.
```

Sweet Talkin' Woman

Words and Music by Jeff Lynne

Melody:

Sweet talk - in' wom - an,

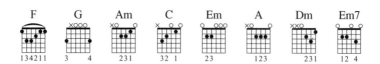

Intro

F	G	Am		F	G	C	

F   G   Am   F   G   C
Sweet talkin' woman, where did you go?

Verse 1

         C
I was searchin' (Searchin'.) on a one way street.

      Am   F
I was hopin' (Hopin'.) for a chance to meet.

      Em   A
I was waitin' for the opera - tor on the line.

Pre-Chorus 1

Dm   Em   Dm
  (She's gone so ___ long.) What can I do?

            Em
(Where could she ___ be?) No, no, no.

F   G   Am
Don't know what I'm gonna do,

   F   G   C   G
I gotta get back ___ to you.

Chorus 1

           C
You gotta slow down, (Slow down.)

Am   Em
Sweet talkin' woman. (Slow down.)

F   Em7
  You got me runnin', (Run, run.)

F   G
  You got me searchin'.

C   Am   Em
Hold on, (Hold on.) sweet talkin' lover. (Hold on.)

F   Em7   F   G
  It's so sad if that's __ the way it's over.

F   G   Am   F
Sweet talkin' woman.

Verse 2

       G   C
I was… (Walkin'.) Many days go by.

     Am   F
I was thinkin' (Thinkin'.) 'bout the lonely nights.

     Em   A
Com-munication break - down all around.

Pre-Chorus 2   *Repeat Pre-Chorus 1*

Chorus 2

           C
You gotta slow down, (Slow down.)

Am   Em
Sweet talkin' woman. (Slow down.)

F   Em7
  You got me runnin', (Run, run.)

F   G
  You got me searchin'.

C   Am   Em
Hold on, (Hold on.) sweet talkin' lover. (Hold on.)

F   Em7   F   G
  It's so sad if that's __ the way it's over.

F   G   Am
Sweet talkin' woman.

Verse 3	**C** I've been livin' (Livin'.) on a dead end street.
	Am　　　　　　**F** I've been askin' (Kindly.) ev'ry-body I meet.
	Em　　　**A** Insufficient da - ta comin' through.
Pre-Chorus 3	*Repeat Pre-Chorus 1*
Chorus 3	**C** You gotta slow down, (Slow down.)
	Am　　　**Em** Sweet talkin' woman. (Slow down.)
	F　　　　**Em7** 　You got me runnin', (Run, run.)
	F　　**G** 　You got me searchin'.
	C　　　　　　　**Am**　　　**Em** Hold on, (Hold on.) sweet talkin' lover. (Hold on.)
	F　　**Em7**　　**F**　　　**G** 　It's so sad if that's ___ the way it's over.
	F　**G**　**Am**　　**G** Sweet talkin' woman.
Chorus 4	**C**　　　　　　　**Am**　　　**Em** Slow down, (Slow down.) sweet talkin' woman. (Slow down.)
	F　　　　**Em7**　**F**　　　**G** 　You got me runnin',　you got me searchin'.
	C　　　　　　　**Am**　　　**Em** Hold on, (Hold on.) sweet talkin' lover. (Hold on.)
	F　　**Em7**　　**F**　　　**G** 　It's so sad if that's ___ the way it's over.
Outro-Chorus	*Repeat Chorus 4 till fade*

Tangled Up in Blue

Words and Music by Bob Dylan

Melody:

Ear-ly one morn-in' the sun ___ was shin-in', ___

A   Asus4   G/A   D   E   F#m   G

Intro   ‖: A   **Asus4** | A   **Asus4** :‖

Verse 1

A   **G/A**   **A**   **G/A**
Early one mornin' the sun ___ was shinin', I was lay'n' in bed,

A   **G/A**   **D**
Wond'rin' if she'd changed at all, if her hair was still red.

A   **G/A**   **A**   **G/A**
Her folks, they said our lives ___ together sure was gonna be rough.

      A   **G/A**
They never did like Mama's homemade dress,

      D
Papa's bank book wasn't big enough.

      E   **F#m**   **A**   **D**
And I was standin' on the side of the road, rain ___ fallin' on my shoes.

      E   **F#m**
     Heading up for the East ___ Coast,

      A   **D**   **E**
Lord knows I've paid some dues ___ gettin' through;

      G   **D**   **A**
Tangled up in blue.

Interlude 1   *Repeat Intro*

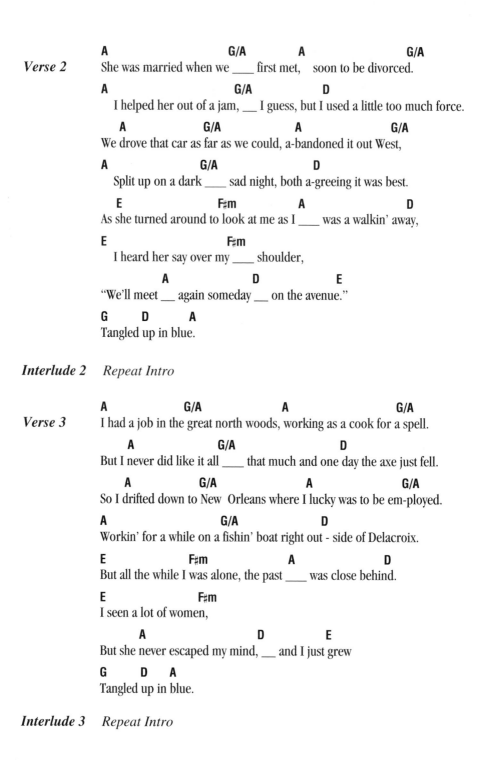

Verse 2

```
    A                      G/A          A              G/A
She was married when we ___ first met,   soon to be divorced.
    A                      G/A              D
    I helped her out of a jam, ___ I guess, but I used a little too much force.
      A            G/A          A            G/A
    We drove that car as far as we could, a-bandoned it out West,
    A            G/A              D
    Split up on a dark ___ sad night, both a-greeing it was best.
      E                   F♯m           A              D
    As she turned around to look at me as I ___ was a walkin' away,
    E                      F♯m
    I heard her say over my ___ shoulder,
              A              D              E
    "We'll meet ___ again someday ___ on the avenue."
    G      D      A
    Tangled up in blue.
```

Interlude 2   *Repeat Intro*

Verse 3

```
    A                  G/A              A                  G/A
I had a job in the great north woods, working as a cook for a spell.
      A              G/A              D
    But I never did like it all ___ that much and one day the axe just fell.
      A            G/A              A                G/A
    So I drifted down to New  Orleans where I lucky was to be em-ployed.
    A                  G/A              D
    Workin' for a while on a fishin' boat right out - side of Delacroix.
    E            F♯m              A              D
    But all the while I was alone, the past ___ was close behind.
    E                      F♯m
    I seen a lot of women,
          A                  D          E
    But she never escaped my mind, ___ and I just grew
    G      D      A
    Tangled up in blue.
```

Interlude 3   *Repeat Intro*

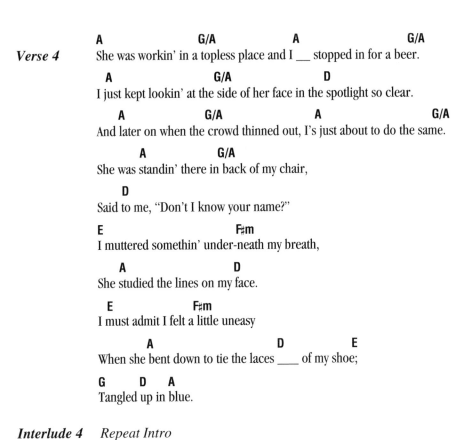

Verse 4

```
      A                 G/A               A                    G/A
      She was workin' in a topless place and I __ stopped in for a beer.

      A                 G/A               D
      I just kept lookin' at the side of her face in the spotlight so clear.

        A                 G/A               A                    G/A
      And later on when the crowd thinned out, I's just about to do the same.

            A             G/A
      She was standin' there in back of my chair,

            D
      Said to me, "Don't I know your name?"

      E                           F♯m
      I muttered somethin' under-neath my breath,

            A                   D
      She studied the lines on my face.

        E               F♯m
      I must admit I felt a little uneasy

              A                       D               E
      When she bent down to tie the laces ___ of my shoe;

      G     D     A
      Tangled up in blue.
```

Interlude 4   *Repeat Intro*

	A G/A A G/A

Verse 5

        A   **G/A**   **A**   **G/A**
She lit a burner on ___ the stove and offered me a pipe.

        A   **G/A**
"I thought you'd never say hel-lo," she said,

        D
"You look like the silent type."

                A   **G/A**   **A**   **G/A**
Then she opened up a book of poems and handed it to me,

A   **G/A**   **D**
Written by an I-talian poet from the thirteenth century.

        E   **F♯m**
And ev'ry one of them words ___ rang true

            A   **D**
And glowed __ like burnin' coal.

E   **F♯m**
Pourin' off of ev'ry page

        A   **D**   **E**
Like it was written in my soul from me to you;

G   **D**   **A**
Tangled up in blue.

Interlude 5   *Repeat Intro*

Verse 6

A	G/A	A	G/A

I lived with them on Montague Street in a basement down the stairs.

A	G/A	D

There was music in the ca-fés at night and revo-lution in the air.

A	G/A

Then he started into dealin' with slaves

A	G/A

And something inside of him died.

A	G/A	D

She had to sell ev'rything ___ she owned and ___ froze up inside.

E	F♯m	A	D

And when it finally, the bottom fell out I __ became with-drawn.

E	F♯m

The only thing I knew how to do

A	D	E

Was to keep on keepin' on like a bird that flew;

G	D	A

Tangled up in blue.

Interlude 6   *Repeat Intro*

Verse 7

A	G/A	A	G/A

So now I'm goin' back again, I got to get to her some-how.

A	G/A	D

All the people we used to know, they're an il-lusion to me now.

A	G/A	A	G/A

Some are mathema-ticians; some are carpenter's wives.

A	G/A

Don't know how it all got started,

D

I don't know what they're doin' with their lives.

E	F♯m	A	D

But me, I'm still on the road, headin' for another joint.

E	F♯m

We always did feel the same,

A	D	E

We just saw it from a diff'rent point of view;

G	D	A

Tangled up in blue.

Interlude 7   *Repeat Intro*

Outro   *Repeat Verse 7 (Instrumental)*

Tears in Heaven

Words and Music by
Eric Clapton and Will Jennings

Melody:

Would you know my name

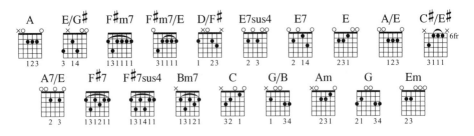

Intro | A   E/G♯ F♯m7 | F♯m7/E | D/F♯   E7sus4 E7| A |

Verse 1

A   E/G♯   F♯m7   F♯m7/E
Would you know my name

D/F♯   A   E   A/E   E7
If I saw you in heav-en?

A   E/G♯ F♯m7   F♯m7/E
Would it be the same

D/F♯   A/E   E   A/E   E7
If I saw you in heav-en?

Chorus 1

F♯m7   C♯/E♯
I must be strong

A7/E   F♯7
And carry on,

F♯7sus4 F♯7   Bm7
'Cause   I   know

                E7sus4
I don't belong

            A   E/G♯ F♯m7   F♯m7/E   D/F♯   E7sus4   E7   A
Here in heav-en.

GUITAR CHORD SONGBOOK

Verse 2

```
A            E/G#    F#m7    F#m7/E
        Would you hold my hand
D/F#   A            E    A/E   E7
        If I saw you in heav-en?
A            E/G#    F#m7    F#m7/E
        Would ya help me stand
D/F#   A/E            E    A/E   E7
        If I saw you in heav-en?
```

Chorus 2

```
F#m7                C#/E#
        I'll find my way
A7/E                        F#7
        Through night and day
F#7sus4   F#7    Bm7
'Cause     I    know
                        E7sus4
I just can't stay
                A   E/G#  F#m7    F#m7/E   D/F#   E7sus4   E7   A
Here in heav-en.
```

Bridge

```
C          G/B    Am
        Time can bring ya down,
            D/F#            G   D/F#  Em   D/F#  G
Time can bend your knees.
C          G/B        Am
        Time can break your heart,
        D/F#            G
Have ya beggin' please,
D/F#            E   A/E  E7
        Beggin' please.
```

Interlude   *Repeat Verse 2 (Instrumental)*

                        F#m7   C#/E#
Chorus 3   Beyond the door

                        A7/E   F#7
                        There's peace, I'm sure,

                        F#7sus4 F#7   Bm7
                        And   I   know

                                         E7sus4
                        There'll be no more

                                    A   E/G# F#m7 F#m7/E D/F# E7sus4 E7 A
                        Tears in heav-en.

Verse 3   *Repeat Verse 1*

                        F#m7   C#/E#
Chorus 4   I must be strong

                        A7/E   F#7
                        And carry on,

                        F#7sus4   F#7   Bm7
                        'Cause   I   know

                                    E7sus4
                        I don't belong

                                    A   E/G# F#m7
                        Here in heav-en.

                        F#m7/E   Bm7
                        'Cause I know

                                    E7sus4
                        I don't belong

                                    A   E/G# F#m7 F#m7/E D/F# E7sus4 E7 A
                        Here in heav-en.

3 AM

Lyrics by Rob Thomas
Music by Rob Thomas,
Brian Yale, John Leslie Goff
and John Joseph Stanley

Melody:

She says it's cold _____ out - side _ and she hands _ me my rain-

(Capo 1st fret)

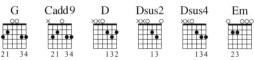

Intro

| G   Cadd9 | | G   Cadd9 | |
| G   Cadd9 | G   Cadd9 | G   Cadd9 | G   Cadd9 |

Verse 1

D   Cadd9
She says it's cold ____ outside
                       G
And she hands me my rain - coat.
D   Cadd9   G   Cadd9   G   Cadd9
She's always worried about things like that.
D   Cadd9
Well, she says it's all ____ gonna end
                       G   Cadd9   G   Cadd9
And it might as well be my ____ fault.
        D   Dsus2   Cadd9
And she only sleeps when it's rain - in'.
        Dsus4   D   Cadd9
And she screams, and her voice ____ is strainin'.

Chorus 1

        G   D Cadd9
She says, "Baby,   it's three a.m.,
        D   G   D   Cadd9
I __ must be lone - ly."
D   G   D   Cadd9
When she says, "Baby,   well, I can't help
        D   Em   D
But be scared of it all ____ some-times."
Cadd9
And the rain's gonna wash away, I believe it.

ACOUSTIC ROCK

Interlude 1 ‖: G   Cadd9 | G   Cadd9 :‖

                    D   Cadd9

Verse 2   But she's gotta little ___ bit of somethin',

                                   G

        God, it's better than noth - in'.

        D   Cadd9

        And in her color por-trait world

                                  G Cadd9   G   Cadd9

        She believes that she's got it all,   all.

        D   Cadd9

        She swears the moon ___ don't hang

                            G   Cadd9   G   Cadd9

        Quite as high as it used to.

                      D   Dsus2   Cadd9

        And she only sleeps when it's rain - in'.

                    Dsus4   D   Cadd9

        And she screams, and her voice ___ is strainin'.

                        G   D Cadd9

Chorus 2   She says, "Baby,   it's three a.m.,

            D   G   D   Cadd9

        I ___ must be lone - ly."

        D   G   D Cadd9

        When she says, "Baby,   well, I can't help

            D   Em   D

        But be scared of it all ___ some-times."

        Cadd9

        And the rain's gonna wash away, I believe, yes

Interlude 2 |G   Cadd9 |G   Cadd9 |G   Cadd9 |G   Cadd9 |

Verse 3

     D   **Cadd9**
Well, she believes ___ that life is made up

                 G   **Cadd9**   **G**   **Cadd9**
Of all that you're used ___ to.

                 Cadd9
And the clock on the wall ___ has been stuck at three

     G   **Cadd9**   **G**   **Cadd9**
For days and days.

     D   **Cadd9**
She thinks that hap - piness is a mat

             G   **Cadd9**   **G**   **Cadd9**
That sits on her door - way,   yeah.

       D   **C**
But outside it stopped rainin'.

Chorus 3

         G   **D** **Cadd9**
Yeah, but she says, "Baby,   it's three a.m.,

     D   **G**   **D**   **Cadd9**
I __ must be lone - ly."

     D   **G**   **D** **Cadd9**
When she says, "Baby,   well, I can't help

     D   **Em**   **D**
But be scared of it all ___ some-times."

Cadd9
And the rain's gonna wash away,

      G   **D**   **Cadd9**
I believe   this.

         D   **G**   **D** **Cadd9**
Well, it's three a.m., I must be lone - ly.

       D
Whenev-er she says,

 G   **D** **Cadd9**
  "Baby,   well, I can't help

     D   **Em** **D** **Cadd9**
But be scared of it all ___ some-times."

Time for Me to Fly

Words and Music by Kevin Cronin

Open D tuning:
(low to high) D-A-D-F#-A-D

Melody:

I've been a - round _ for _ you, I've

D   Aadd4   Gadd9   Gadd9/D   A5

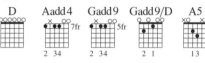

Intro ‖: D   Gadd9 | Aadd4   Gadd9 :‖

Verse 1

D
I've been around for you,

Aadd4
I've been up and down for you,

Gadd9   **D Gadd9/D D   Gadd9/D D**
But I__ just can't get any relief.

I've swallowed my pride for you,

Aadd4
Lived and lied for you,

Gadd9   **D Gadd9/D D   Gadd9/D D**
But a you still make me feel like a thief.

Aadd4
You got me stealin' your love away

Gadd9   D
'Cause a you never give it.

Aadd4
Peelin' the years away

Gadd9   D
And a we can't re-live it.

Gadd9   D
Oh, I make you laugh,

Gadd9   D
And a you make me cry.

Aadd4
I believe it's time for me to fly.

‖: D   Gadd9 | Aadd4   Gadd9   :‖

Verse 2

D
You said we'd work it out,

   Aadd4
You said that you had no doubt,

   Gadd9   **D**   **Gadd9/D** **D** **Gadd9/D**
That deep down we were really in love.

D
Oh, but I'm tired of holdin' on

   Aadd4
To feelin' I know is gone.

Gadd9   **D**   **Gadd9/D** **D** **Gadd9/D**
  I do believe that I've had enough.

   D   **Aadd4**
I've had e-nough of the falseness

     Gadd9   **D**
Of a worn - out re-lation.

  Aadd4
E-nough of the jealousy

    Gadd9   **D**
And the intolera - tion.

   Gadd9   **D**
Oh, I make you laugh,

    Gadd9   **D**
And a you make me cry.

Aadd4   **D**   **Gadd9**   **D** **N.C.**
  I believe it's time for me to fly.

Chorus 1

                Aadd4   **Gadd9**   **D**
(Time for me to fly.)

                       Oh, I've got to set__ myself free.

                Aadd4   **Gadd9**   **D**
(Time for me to fly.)

                   Ah, that's just how it's a got to be.

Gadd9   **Aadd4**
I know it hurts to say good-bye,

                        Gadd9   **Aadd4**
But it's time for me to fly.

Interlude | D | | Gadd9| |
                  | Aadd4 | | D | |

                         Aadd4   **Gadd9**   **D**
Chorus 2   (Time for me to fly.)

                      Oh, I've got to set__ myself free.

                      Aadd4   **Gadd9 D**
(Time for me to fly.)

                      Ah, that's just how it's a got to   be.

Gadd9   **Aadd4**
I know it hurts to say good-bye,

                      Gadd9   **Aadd4**
But it's time for me to fly.

                  Gadd9   **A5**
It's time for me to fly,__ ee-i, ee-i.

                D
It's time for me to fly.

          Gadd9   **Aadd4**
(It's time for me to fly.)

          Gadd9   **D**
It's time for me to fly.

                Aadd4
(It's time for me to fly.)

          Gadd9   **D**
It's time for me to fly.

            Gadd9   **Aadd4**   **Gadd9 D**
(It's time for me to fly.)

                  Babe,__ it's time for me to fly.

Time in a Bottle

Words and Music by Jim Croce

Melody:

If I could save __ time in a

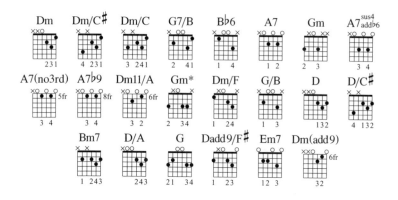

Intro

Dm	Dm/C♯	Dm/C	G7/B	
B♭6	A7 Gm	A7 A7$^{sus4}_{add♭6}$ A7(no3rd)	
A7♭9 Dm11/A A7(no3rd)	

Verse 1

      Dm   Dm/C♯   Dm/C G7/B
If I could save ____ time in a bottle,

    B♭6   A7 Gm
The first thing that I'd like to do

| A7 A7$^{sus4}_{add♭6}$ A7(no3rd) | A7♭9 Dm11/A A7(no3rd) |

    Dm   Dm/C
Is to save ev'ry-day

      B♭6   Gm*   Dm/F
Till e-ternity pass - es away

     Gm*   A7 G/B A7(no3rd) A7
Just to spend them with you.

Verse 2

Dm   Dm/C♯   Dm/C G7/B
If I could make days last for-ever,

B♭6   A7 Gm
If words could make wish-es come

A7 A7$^{sus4}_{add♭6}$ A7(no3rd) A7♭9 Dm11/A A7(no3rd)
True;

  Dm   Dm/C
I'd save ev'ry-day

  B♭6   Gm*
Like a treasure and then,

  Dm/F   Gm*   A7 G/B A7(no3rd) A7
A-gain I would spend them with you.

Chorus 1

       D   D/C♯
But there never seems to be enough time

  Bm7   D/A   G
To do the things you wanna do once you find them.

| Dadd9/F♯ | Em7 | A7 G/B A7(no3rd) |

    D   D/C♯
I've looked around e-nough to know

  Bm7   D/A   G
That you're the one I want to go through time with.

| Dadd9/F♯ | Em7 | A7 G/B A7(no3rd) |

Interlude   *Repeat Intro*

Verse 3
      Dm   **Dm/C♯**   **Dm/C** **G7/B**
If I had a box just for wishes,

      B♭6   **A7** **Gm**
And dreams that had never __ come

A7 **A7$_{add♭6}^{sus4}$** **A7(no3rd)** **A7♭9** **Dm11/A** **A7(no3rd)**
True;

      Dm   **Dm/C**
The box would be empty

      B♭6   **Gm***   **Dm/F**
Ex-cept for the mem'ry of how

         Gm*   **A7** **G/B** **A7(no3rd)** **A7**
They were answered by you.

Chorus 2   *Repeat Chorus 1*

Outro   ‖: **Dm(add9)** | :‖ *Play 3 times*

Torn

Words and Music by Phil Thornalley,
Scott Cutler and Anne Previn

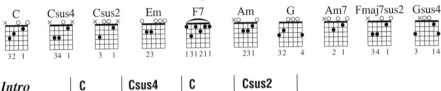

(Capo 5th fret)

C   Csus4   Csus2   Em   F7   Am   G   Am7   Fmaj7sus2   Gsus4

Intro | C | Csus4 | C | Csus2 |

Verse 1
> **C**
> I thought I saw a man brought to life.
>
> **Em**
> He was warm, he came around
>
> **F7**
> Like he was dig - nified.
>
> He showed me what it was to cry.
>
> **C**
> Well, you couldn't be that man I adored.
>
> **Em**
> You don't seem to know, seem to care
>
> **F7**
> What your heart is for.
>
> I don't know him anymore.
>
> **Am**
> There's nothin' where he used to lie.
>
> **G**
> My conversation has run dry.
>
> **Em**
> That's what's going on.
>
> **G**   **C**
> Nothing's fine, I'm torn.

Chorus 1

     C   **G**
     I'm all out of faith,

        Am7
     This is how I feel.

             Fmaj7sus2
     I'm cold and I am shamed

           C
     Lying naked on the floor.

          G   **Am7**
     Illusion never changed__ into something real.

     I'm wide awake

     Fmaj7sus2   **C**
     And I__ can see the perfect sky is torn.

         G
     You're a little late,

        Am7   **Fmaj7sus2**
     I'm already torn.

Verse 2

     C
       So, I guess the fortune teller's right.

     Em
       I should've seen just what was there

        F7
     And not some holy light.

     But you crawled beneath my veins, and now

     Am
     I don't care, I have no luck.

     G
       I don't miss it all that much.

     Em   **G**
       There's just so many things

          C
     That I can't touch. I'm torn.

                        C   G
Chorus 2   I'm all out of faith,
                                      Am7
                This is how I feel.
                                              Fmaj7sus2
                I'm cold and I am shamed
                                          C
                Lying naked on the floor.
                                      G   Am7
                Illusion never changed__ into something real.

                I'm wide awake
                    Fmaj7sus2   C
                And I__ can see the perfect sky is torn.
                                  G
                You're a little late,
                                  Am7   Fmaj7sus2
                I'm already torn.
                Am7   Fmaj7sus2
                Torn.

                    Am   C   G
Interlude   Oo, oo.

Verse 3

         Am
There's nothing where he used to lie.

  G
     My inspiration has run dry.

  Em
     That's what's going on.

  G
     Nothing's right, I'm torn.

Chorus 3   ***Repeat Chorus 1***

           G
Outro   I'm all out of faith,

         Am7
This is how I feel.

            Fmaj7sus2
I'm cold and I'm ashamed,

           C
Bound and broken on the floor.

       G
You're a little late.

       Am7   **Fmaj7sus2**
I'm already torn.

Am7   **G**   **Gsus4**
Torn.   Oh.

| **C** | | **G** | | **Am7** | | **Fmaj7sus2** |

Tropicalia

Words and Music by Beck Hansen

Melody:

Oh, when they   beat

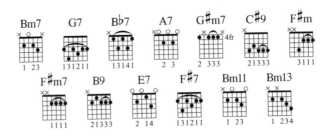

Intro   ‖:Bm7 G7 | |Bm7 G7 | :‖

Verse 1

 Bm7   G7
Oh, when they beat upon a broken guitar,

 Bm7   G7
And all the streets, they reek of tropical charms,

 Bm7   G7
The embas-sies lie in hideous shards

 B♭7   A7
Where tourists snore and de-cay.

Verse 2

 Bm7   G7
Oh, when they dance in a reptile blaze,

 Bm7   G7   Bm7
You wear a mask, an e-quatorial haze into the past,

 G7   B♭7   A7
A colonial maze where there's no more confetti to throw.

GUITAR CHORD SONGBOOK

Chorus 1

       G♯m7   **C♯9**   **G♯m7**
You wouldn't know what to say to yourself.

       C♯9   **F♯m**
Love is a poverty you couldn't sell.

       F♯m7 B9   **E7**   **G7**   **F♯7**
Misery waits in vague hotels ____ to be evict-ed.

Interlude 1 |**Bm7** **G7** | |**Bm7** **G7** | |

Verse 3

               Bm7   **G7**
You're out of luck, you're sing-ing funeral songs

       Bm7   **G7**
To the studs, they're an-abolic and bronze.

          Bm7   **G7**
They seem to strut in their millenial fogs

       B♭7   **A7**
Till they ____ fall down and de-flate.

Chorus 2   *Repeat Chorus 1*

Interlude 2   *Repeat Interlude 1*

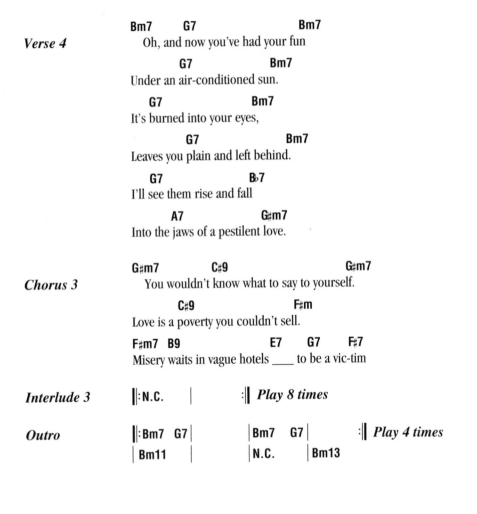

Verse 4

    Bm7   **G7**   **Bm7**
Oh, and now you've had your fun

       G7   **Bm7**
Under an air-conditioned sun.

   G7   **Bm7**
It's burned into your eyes,

      G7   **Bm7**
Leaves you plain and left behind.

   G7   **B♭7**
I'll see them rise and fall

    A7   **G♯m7**
Into the jaws of a pestilent love.

Chorus 3

   G♯m7   **C♯9**   **G♯m7**
You wouldn't know what to say to yourself.

    C♯9   **F♯m**
Love is a poverty you couldn't sell.

F♯m7 B9   **E7** **G7** **F♯7**
Misery waits in vague hotels ___ to be a vic-tim

Interlude 3   ‖: N.C. | :‖ *Play 8 times*

Outro   ‖: **Bm7 G7** | | **Bm7 G7** | :‖ *Play 4 times*
       | **Bm11** | | **N.C.** | **Bm13**

Wake Up Little Susie

Melody:

Words and Music by
Boudleaux Bryant and Felice Bryant

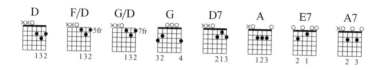

Intro ‖: D |F/D G/D F/D :‖

Chorus 1

D   F/D G/D F/D D
Wake up, little Susie, wake up.

                                      F/D G/D F/D D
Wake up, little Susie, wake up.

Verse 1

        G   D7   G
We've both been sound asleep.

        D7   G
Wake up little Susie and weep.

        D7   G   D7
The movie's o - ver, it's four o-clock,

        G   D7   G
And we're in trouble deep.

ACOUSTIC ROCK

Chorus 2

              A
Wake up, little Susie,

G   **A**
  Wake up, little Susie.

                     E7   **A**
Well, what are we gonna tell your ma - ma?

                E7   **A**
What are we gonna tell your pa?

                E7   **A**
What are we gonna tell our friends

When they say, "Ooh la la?"

         A7   **D**
Wake up, _____ little Susie.

A7   **D**
  Wake up, little Susie.

Bridge

D
  Well, I told your mama that you'd be in by ten.

D7   **G**
  Well, Susie baby, looks like we goofed again.

             A
Wake up, little Susie.

G   **A**
  Wake up, little Susie.

A7 N.C.   **D**
  We gotta go home.

Interlude   ‖: **D** | **F/D**   **G/D**   **F/D** :‖

Chorus 3   *Repeat Chorus 1*

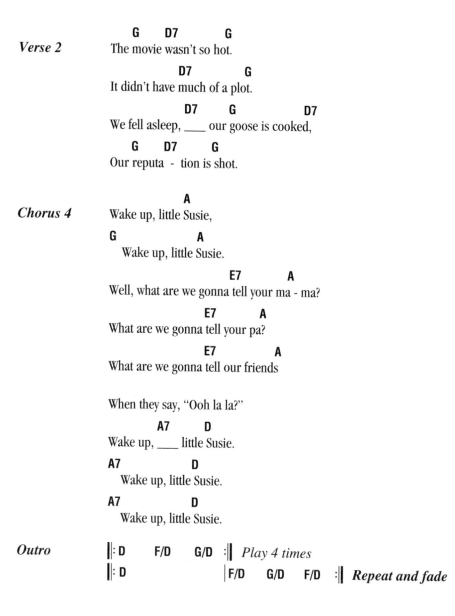

Verse 2

```
        G      D7        G
The movie wasn't so hot.
                  D7        G
It didn't have much of a plot.
                      D7    G           D7
We fell asleep, ___ our goose is cooked,
        G    D7    G
Our reputa - tion is shot.
```

Chorus 4

```
                        A
Wake up, little Susie,
G               A
   Wake up, little Susie.
                          E7      A
Well, what are we gonna tell your ma - ma?
                    E7      A
What are we gonna tell your pa?
                      E7          A
What are we gonna tell our friends

When they say, "Ooh la la?"
              A7      D
Wake up, ___ little Susie.
A7              D
   Wake up, little Susie.
A7              D
   Wake up, little Susie.
```

Outro

```
‖: D      F/D      G/D :‖  Play 4 times
‖: D                  |F/D    G/D    F/D :‖  Repeat and fade
```

Two Out of Three Ain't Bad

Words and Music by Jim Steinman

Ba - by, we can talk all ___ night, ___

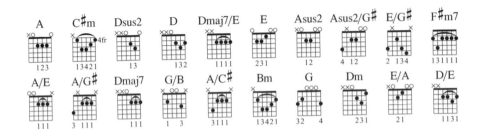

Intro | A | C#m | Dsus2 D | Dmaj7/E E |

Verse 1

    Asus2   **Asus2/G#**
Baby, we can talk all night,

    D   **Dsus2**   **A**
But that ain't getting us no - where.

       E/G#   **F#m7**
I told you ev'rything I possibly can,

Dmaj7/E   **E**
There's nothing left inside of here.

    Asus2   **Asus2/G#**
And maybe you can cry all night,

    D   **Dsus2**   **A**   **Asus2**
But that'll never change the way ___ that I feel.

A/E   **A/G#**   **F#m7**
The snow is really piling up outside,

Dmaj7   **E**
I wish you wouldn't make me leave here.

Pre-Chorus 1

```
D                    E      A       G/B  A/C#
I poured it on and I poured ___ it out.

D               E      A       Bm  C#m
I tried to show you just how much I care.

D                    E      A      F#m7
I'm tired of words and I'm too hoarse to shout.

G
But you've been cold to me so long,

            D                E
I'm crying icicles instead of tears.

      D      E    D     E
And all I can do is keep on telling you,
```

Chorus 1

```
      A              E/G#
I want you, (I want you.)

   F#m7
I need you, (I need you.)

              D      E     C#m       F#m7
But there ain't no way I'm ev - er gonna love you.

      Bm
Now, don't be sad,

      D              Dm      F#m7
'Cause two outta three ___ ain't bad.

      Bm
Now, don't be sad,

      D              Dm         A    E/A  A  G/B  A/C#
'Cause two outta three ___ ain't bad.
```

Bridge

      D   **E A**
You'll never find your gold on a sandy beach.

E   **D**   **E A**
You'll never drill for oil on a city street.

E   **D**   **E**   **A**
I know you're looking for a ru-by in a mountain of rocks,

        G
But there ain't no Coupe de Ville

             E
Hiding at the bottom of a Crackerjack box.

C♯m   **D**
I can't lie, I can't tell you that I'm something I'm not.

            C♯m
No matter how I try, I'll never be able to give you something,

D   **E**
Something that I just haven't got.

Verse 2

       Asus2   **Asus2/G♯**
Well, there's only one girl that I will ever love,

        D   **Dsus2** **A/E** **Asus2**
And that was so many years _____ ago.

    A   **A/G♯**   **F♯m7**
And though I know I'll never get her out of my heart,

   Dmaj7/E   **E**
She never loved me back, ooh, ____ I know.

   Asus2   **Asus2/G♯**
Well, I re-member how she left me on a stormy night.

    D   **Dsus2** **A** **Asus2**
Oh, she kissed me and got out of our bed.

      A/E   **A/G♯**   **F♯m7**
And though I pleaded and I begged her not to walk out that door,

   Dmaj7   **E**
She packed her bags and turned right away.

    D/E **E**   **D/E** **E**   **D/E** **E**
And she kept on telling me, she kept on telling me, she kept on telling me,

Chorus 2

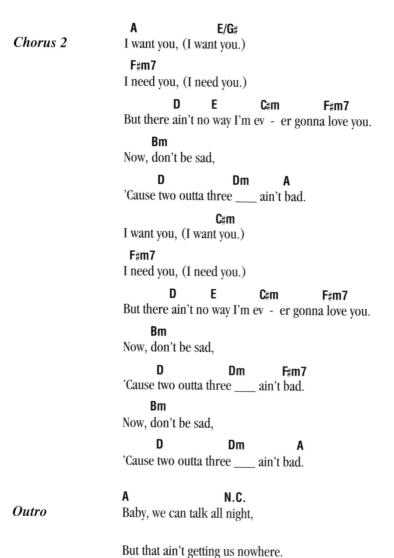

    A   E/G♯
I want you, (I want you.)

  F♯m7
I need you, (I need you.)

     D   E   C♯m   F♯m7
But there ain't no way I'm ev - er gonna love you.

  Bm
Now, don't be sad,

    D   Dm A
'Cause two outta three ___ ain't bad.

       C♯m
I want you, (I want you.)

  F♯m7
I need you, (I need you.)

     D   E   C♯m   F♯m7
But there ain't no way I'm ev - er gonna love you.

   Bm
Now, don't be sad,

    D   Dm   F♯m7
'Cause two outta three ___ ain't bad.

   Bm
Now, don't be sad,

    D   Dm   A
'Cause two outta three ___ ain't bad.

Outro

  A   N.C.
Baby, we can talk all night,

But that ain't getting us nowhere.

When the Children Cry

Words and Music by Mike Tramp and Vito Bratta

Melody:

Lit - tle   child___

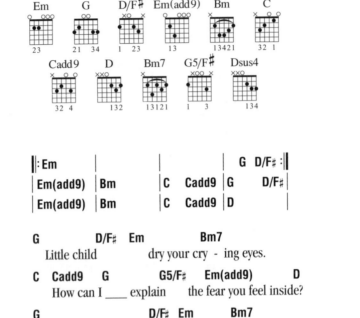

Intro

‖: Em | | | G D/F♯ :‖
| Em(add9) | Bm |C Cadd9 |G D/F♯|
| Em(add9) | Bm |C Cadd9 |D |

Verse 1

G   D/F♯ Em   Bm7
Little child   dry your cry - ing eyes.

C Cadd9 G   G5/F♯ Em(add9)   D
How can I ___ explain the fear you feel inside?

G   D/F♯ Em Bm7
'Cause you were born into this evil world.

C   Cadd9 G   G5/F♯ Em(add9)   D
Where man is kill - ing man and no one knows just why.

Pre-Chorus 1

C   Bm
What have we become?

Em(add9)   Bm
Just look what we ___ have done.

C Cadd9 G   G5/F♯
All that we've ___ destroyed

Em(add9)   D Dsus4 D
You must build a-gain.

```
                  Em(add9)  Bm           C     Cadd9  G
Chorus 1     When the children cry ____ let them know we tried.

                  G5/F♯   Em(add9)  Bm          C  Cadd9     D
             'Cause when the children sing ____ then the new world begins.


                  G          D/F♯  Em       Bm7
Verse 2         Little child       you must show the way

             C   Cadd9 G      G5/F♯   Em(add9) D
             To a bet - ter day ____ for all the     young.

             G                    D/F♯  Em       Bm7
             'Cause you were born       for the world to see

             C   Cadd9   G        G5/F♯  Em(add9)    D
             That we all can live with love _____ and ___ peace.


                  C          Bm
Pre-Chorus 2   No more presidents.

             Em(add9)        Bm
             And all the wars ____ will end.

             C   Cadd9  G       G5/F♯  Em(add9)    D  Dsus4  D
             One unit - ed world           under God.


                  Em(add9)  Bm           C     Cadd9  G
Chorus 2     When the children cry ____ let them know we tried.

                  G5/F♯   Em(add9)  Bm          C  Cadd9     D  Dsus4  D
             'Cause when the children sing __ then the new world begins.


Guitar Solo    Repeat Verse 1 (Instrumental)

Pre-Chorus 3   Repeat Pre-Chorus 1

Pre-Chorus 4   Repeat Pre-Chorus 2


                  Em(add9)  Bm           C     Cadd9  G
Chorus 3     When the children cry ____ let them know we tried.

                  G5/F♯    Em(add9)  Bm          C   Cadd9     D
             'Cause when the children fight ____ let them know it ain't right.

             G   G5/F♯   Em(add9)  Bm            C     Cadd9 G
             When the children pray ____ let them know the way.

                       G5/F♯  Em(add9)  Bm            C   Cadd9      D
             'Cause when the     children sing ____ then the new world begins.
```

Wherever You Will Go

Words and Music by Aaron Kamin and Alex Band

Melody:

So late - ly,

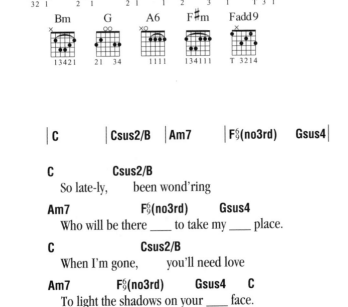

Intro

| C | Csus2/B | Am7 | F⁶₉(no3rd) Gsus4 |

Verse 1

C   Csus2/B
So late-ly,   been wond'ring

Am7   F⁶₉(no3rd)   Gsus4
Who will be there ___ to take my ___ place.

C   Csus2/B
When I'm gone,   you'll need love

Am7   F⁶₉(no3rd)   Gsus4   C
To light the shadows on your ___ face.

     Csus2/B   Am7
If the great - er wave shall fall,

     F⁶₉(no3rd)   Gsus4 C
And fall ___ upon us ___ all,

     Csus2/B   Am7
Then between ___ the sand and stone,

    F⁶₉(no3rd)
Could you make ___ it on your own?

GUITAR CHORD SONGBOOK

Chorus 1

C   Csus2/B
If I could,   then I would,

Am7   Fsus2(maj7) C
I'll go wher-ever you will go.

            Csus2/B
Way up high,   or down low,

Am7   F$^6_9$(no3rd)   Gsus4
I'll go wher-ever you will ___ go.

Verse 2

C   Csus2/B
And maybe   I'll find out

Am7   F$^6_9$(no3rd)   Gsus4   C
A way to make it back some ___ day.

            Csus2/B
Towards you,   to guide you

Am7   F$^6_9$(no3rd)   Gsus4   C
Through the darkest of your ___ days.

       Csus2/B   Am7
If the great - er wave shall fall

       F$^6_9$(no3rd)   Gsus4 C
And fall ___ upon us all,

          Csus2/B   Am7
Well, then I hope there's someone out ___ there who

       F$^6_9$(no3rd)
Can bring me back too.

Chorus 2

C   Csus2/B
If I could,   then I would,

Am7   Fsus2(maj7) C
I'll go wher-ever you will go.

            Csus2/B
Way up high,   or down low,

Am7   Fsus2(maj7)
I'll go wher-ever you will

Bridge

Bm G   A6
Go. Run away with my heart,

F♯m   Bm
Run away with my hope.

G   A6   F♯m
Run away with my love.

Verse 3

C   Csus2/B
I know now   just quite how

Am7   F⅋(no3rd)   Gsus4   C
My life and love ____ might still go ____ on.

              Csus2/B
In your heart,   in your mind,

Am7   F⅋(no3rd)
I'll stay with you   for all of time.

Chorus 3

C   Csus2/B
If I could,   then I would,

Am7   Fsus2(maj7)   C
I'll go wher-ever you will go.

              Csus2/B
Way up high,   or down low,

Am7   Fsus2(maj7)   C
I'll go wher-ever you will go.

              Csus2/B   Am7
If I could turn back time,

              Fsus2(maj7)   C
I'll go wher-ever you will go.

              Csus2/B   Am7
If I could make you mine,

              Fsus2(maj7)   C   Csus2/B   Am7
I'll go wher-ever you will go.

              Fsus2(maj7)   C   Csus2/B   Am7   Fsus2(maj7) Fadd9
I'll go wher-ever you will go.

Wonderwall

Words and Music by Noel Gallagher

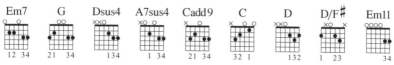

To - day   is gon - na be the day that they're

(Capo 2nd fret)

Em7   G   Dsus4 A7sus4 Cadd9   C   D   D/F♯   Em11

12 34   21 34   1 34   1 34   21 34   32 1   1 32   1 23   34

Intro   ‖: Em7   G | Dsus4   A7sus4 :‖ *Play 4 times*

Verse 1

Em7   G
Today is gon-na be the day

Dsus4   A7sus4
That they're gonna throw it back to you.

Em7   G
By now you should have somehow

Dsus4   A7sus4
Real-ized what you gotta do.

Em7   G
I don't believe that an - ybody

Dsus4   A7sus4   Cadd9 Dsus4 A7sus4
Feels the way I do about you now.

Verse 2

Em7   G
Backbeat, the word is on the street

Dsus4   A7sus4
That the fire in your heart is out.

Em7   G
I'm sure you've heard it all before,

Dsus4   A7sus4
But you never really had a doubt.

Em7   G
I don't believe that an-ybody

Dsus4   A7sus4   Em7 G Dsus4 A7sus4
Feels the way I do about you now.

ACOUSTIC ROCK

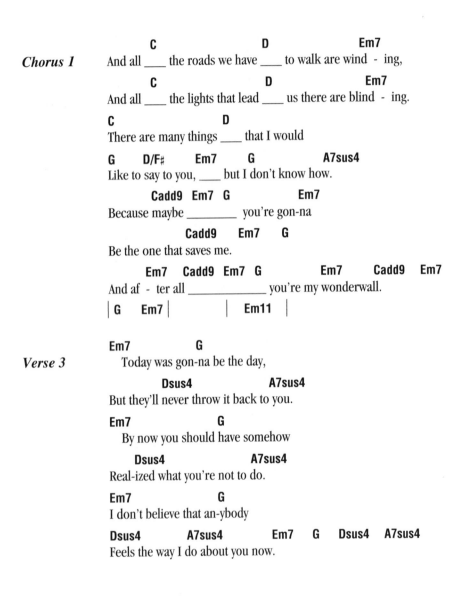

Chorus 1

            C   D   Em7
And all ___ the roads we have ___ to walk are wind - ing,

             C   D   Em7
And all ___ the lights that lead ___ us there are blind - ing.

C   D
There are many things ___ that I would

G   D/F♯   Em7   G   A7sus4
Like to say to you, ___ but I don't know how.

            Cadd9 Em7 G   Em7
Because maybe _____ you're gon-na

             Cadd9   Em7   G
Be the one that saves me.

          Em7   Cadd9 Em7 G   Em7   Cadd9   Em7
And af - ter all _____ you're my wonderwall.

| G   Em7 | | Em11 |

Verse 3

Em7   G
   Today was gon-na be the day,

       Dsus4   A7sus4
But they'll never throw it back to you.

Em7   G
   By now you should have somehow

   Dsus4   A7sus4
Real-ized what you're not to do.

Em7   G
I don't believe that an-ybody

Dsus4   A7sus4   Em7   G   Dsus4   A7sus4
Feels the way I do about you now.

                C   **D**   **Em7**

Chorus 2   And all ___ the roads that lead ___ you there were wind - ing,

                C   **D**   **Em7**
And all ___ the lights that light ___ the way are blind - ing.

C   **D**
There are many things ___ that I would

G   **D/F♯**   **Em7**   **G**   **A7sus4**
Like to say to you, ___ but I don't know how.

       Cadd9 **Em7** **G**   **Em7**
I said maybe _____ you're gon-na

          Cadd9   **Em7**   **G**
Be the one that saves me.

      Em7 **Cadd9** **Em7** **G**
And af - ter all

          Em7   **Cadd9**   **Em7** **G** **Em7**
You're my wonderwall.

       Cadd9 **Em7** **G**   **Em7**
I said maybe _____ you're gon-na

          Cadd9   **Em7** **G**
Be the one that saves me.

      Em7 **Cadd9** **Em7** **G**
And af - ter all

          Em7   **Cadd9**   **Em7** **G** **Em7**
You're my won - derwall.

       Cadd9 **Em7** **G**   **Em7**
I said maybe _____ you're gon-na

          Cadd9   **Em7** **G**
Be the one that saves me.

         Em7   **Cadd9** **Em7** **G**
You're gon-na be the one that saves me.

         Em7   **Cadd9** **Em7** **G** **Em7**
You're gon-na be the one that saves me.

Outro   ‖: **Cadd9**   **Em7**   │ **G**   **Em7**   :‖ *Play 3 times*
          │ **Cadd9**   **Em7**   │ **G**   **Em7**

Yellow

Words and Music by Guy Berryman,
Jon Buckland, Will Champion and Chris Martin

Tuning:
(low to high) E–A–B–G–B–D♯

Melody:

Look at the stars,

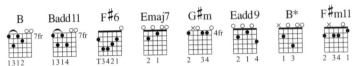

| B | Badd11 | F♯6 | Emaj7 | G♯m | Eadd9 | B* | F♯m11 |

Intro

	B		Badd11	B		Badd11	
	B		Badd11	F♯6			
	Emaj7			B		Badd11	

Verse 1

   B   F♯6
Look at the stars, look how they shine for ____ you,

                Emaj7
And ev'rything you do, ____ yeah, they were all yellow.

   B   F♯6
I came along, I wrote a song for ____ you,

                Emaj7   B
And all the things you do, ____ and it was called yellow.

Badd11   F♯6
So then I took my ____ turn,

             Emaj7
Oh, what a thing to've done,

                B   Badd11   B
And it was all yellow.

Emaj7   G♯m   F♯6   Emaj7
Your skin, ____ oh yeah, your skin and bones,

         G♯m   F♯6
Turn in - to some-thing beautiful.

Emaj7   G♯m   F♯6   Emaj7
And you know, ____ you know I love you so,

Eadd9
You know I love you so.

Interlude 1

```
| B         |        | F♯6    |        |
| Emaj7     |        | B      |        |
```

Verse 2

```
  B                                    F♯6
  I swam across, I jumped across for ___ you,
                         Emaj7
  Oh, what a thing to do, ___ 'cause you were all yellow.
  B              Badd11          F♯6
  I drew a line, I drew a line for ___ you,
                         Emaj7              B      Badd11    B
  Oh, what a thing to do, ___ and it was all yellow.
  Emaj7      G♯m          F♯6            Emaj7
  Your skin, ___ oh yeah, your skin and bones,
       G♯m          F♯6
  Turn in - to some-thing beautiful.
  Emaj7        G♯m         F♯6           Emaj7
  And you know, ___ for you I'd bleed myself dry,
  Eadd9                  B
  For you I'd bleed myself dry.
```

Interlude 2   *Repeat Interlude 1*

Chorus

```
       B                       F♯6
  It's true, look how they shine for you,
                         Emaj7
  Look how they shine for you,
                               B
  Look how they shine for,
                          F♯6
  Look how they shine for you,
                         Emaj7
  Look how they shine for you,

  Look how they shine.
```

Outro

```
  B*
  Look at the stars,
                       F♯m11
  Look how they shine for ___ you,
                       Emaj7
  And all the things that you ___ do.
```

Yesterday

Words and Music by
John Lennon and
Paul McCartney

Yes-ter day,   all my trou-bles seemed so far a-way. _

Tune down 1 step:
(low to high) D-G-C-F-A-D

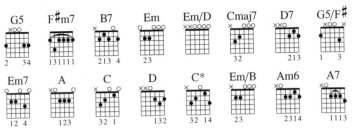

Intro	|G5 | |	

Verse 1

> G5   F♯m7
> Yesterday,

>   B7   Em   Em/D
> All my troubles seemed so far away.

> Cmaj7 D7   G5   G5/F♯
> Now it looks as though they're here to stay.

>   Em7   A   C   G5
> Oh, I believe___ in yes - terday.

Verse 2

> G5   F♯m7
> Suddenly,

>   B7   Em   Em/D
> I'm not half the man I used to be.

> Cmaj7   D7   G5   G5/F♯
> There's a shad - ow hanging over me,

>   Em7   A   C   G5
> Oh, yesterday___ came sud - denly.

Bridge 1

F#m7 B7 Em D C*
Why she had to go

Em/B Am6 D7 G5
I don't know, she wouldn't say.

F#m7 B7 Em D C*
I said some-thing wrong.

Em/B Am6 D7 G5
Now I___ long for yester-day.

Verse 3

G5 F#m7
Yesterday,

B7 Em Em/D
Love was such an easy game to play.

Cmaj7 D7 G5 G5/F#
Now I need a place to hide away.

Em7 A C G5
Oh, I believe___ in yes - terday.

Bridge 2

Repeat Bridge 1

Verse 4

G5 F#m7
Yesterday,

B7 Em Em/D
Love was such an easy game to play.

Cmaj7 D7 G5 G5/F#
Now I need a place to hide away.

Em7 A C G5
Oh, I believe___ in yes - terday.

G A7 C* G5
Mm.

You've Got a Friend

Words and Music by Carole King

When you're down __ and trou - bled,

(Capo 2nd fret)

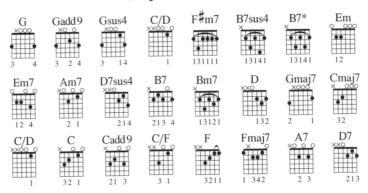

Intro | G Gadd9 Gsus4| C/D | Gsus4 G Gadd9 G| F#m7 B7sus4

Verse 1

         B7*   **Em**   **B7**

When you're down__ and trou - bled,

         Em   **B7**   **Em**   **Em7**

And you need a helping hand,

      Am7   **D7sus4**   **G**   **Gsus4** **G Gsus4 G**

And nothing, whoa, nothing is goin' right,

F#m7   **B7**

Close your eyes and think of me,

      Em   **B7**   **Em**   **Em7**

And soon I will__ be there

      Am7   **Bm7**   **D7sus4**   **D**

To brighten up even your darkest night.

Chorus 1

                  G   **Gmaj7**
You just call___ out my name,

           Cmaj7   **Am7**
And you know wherever I am

D7sus4   **G**   **Gmaj7**
I'll come run - ning, oh yeah, babe,

                  D7sus4
To see you again.

G   **Gmaj7**
Winter, spring, summer or fall,

     Cmaj7   **Em7**
Now, all you got to do is call,

      Cmaj7 **Bm7**   **C/D** **D7sus4**
And I'll be there,___ yeah, yeah, yeah.

              G **Gadd9** **G** **C**   **G**   **F#m7** **B7sus4**
You've got a friend.

Verse 2

      B7   **Em**   **B7**
If the sky___ above___ you

         Em   **B7**   **Em** **Em7**
Should turn___ dark and full of clouds,

       Am7   **D7sus4**   **G** **Gsus4** **G**
And that old North wind should begin to blow,

F#m7   **B7**
  Keep your head togeth - er

     Em   **B7**   **Em** **Em7**   **Am7**
And call my name___ out loud, now.

            Bm7   **D7sus4**
Soon I'll be knock - in' upon your door.

Chorus 2

    Cadd9   **Gmaj7**
    You just call__ out my name,

         Cmaj7   **Am7**
    And you know__ wherever I am,

    D7sus4   **G**   **Gsus4**   **G**
    I'll come run - ning,   oh yes, I will,

             D7sus4
    To see you again.

    G   **Gmaj7**
    Winter, spring, summer or fall,

       Cmaj7   **Em7**
    Yeah, all you got to do is call,

         Cmaj7   **Bm7**   **C/D** **D7sus4**
    And I'll be there, yeah,__ yeah, yeah.

Bridge

        C/F   **F**
    Hey, ain't__ it good to know

    C/D
    That you've got a friend

       G   **Gsus4**   **Gmaj7**
    When people can be__ so cold?

       C
    They'll hurt you,

       Fmaj7
    And desert you.

       Em   **Em7**   **A7**
    Well, they'll take your soul if you let__ them,

         D7sus4   **D7**
    Oh yeah, but don't__ you let them.

Chorus 3
                        Gmaj7
You just call__ out my name,

         Cmaj7   **Am7**
And you know wherever I am,

D7sus4   **G**   **Gsus4**   **G**
  I'll come run-ning

               D7sus4
To see you again.

Oh, babe, don't you know 'bout

G   **Gmaj7**
Winter, spring, summer or fall,

        Cmaj7   **Em7**
Hey, now all you've got to do is call.

        Cmaj7   **Bm7**   **C/D** **D7sus4**
Lord, I'll be__ there, yes, I will.

Outro
                  G **Gadd9 G** **C**
You've got a friend.

           G
You've got a friend, yeah.

C   **G**
  Ain't it good to know you've got__ a friend?

        C
Ain't it good to know

            Gsus4 **G** **Gadd9** **G**
You've got a friend?

        C   **Gsus4** **G** **Gadd9** **G**
Oh,__ yeah, yeah. You've got a friend.

'39

Words and Music by Brian May

Tune up 1/2 step:
(low to high) F–Bb–Eb–Ab–C–F

Melody:

In the year __ of thir - ty - nine, __ as-sem-bled here __

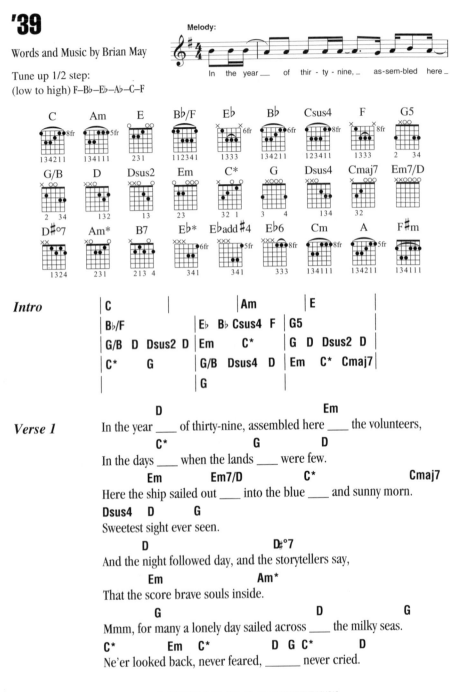

Intro

C			Am	E	
Bb/F			Eb Bb Csus4 F	G5	
G/B D Dsus2 D	Em C*	G D Dsus2 D
C* G	G/B Dsus4 D	Em C* Cmaj7
	G	

Verse 1

           D   **Em**
In the year ___ of thirty-nine, assembled here ___ the volunteers,
       C*   **G**   **D**
In the days ___ when the lands ___ were few.
    Em   **Em7/D**   **C***   **Cmaj7**
Here the ship sailed out ___ into the blue ___ and sunny morn.
Dsus4 D   G
Sweetest sight ever seen.
       D   **D#°7**
And the night followed day, and the storytellers say,
      Em   **Am***
That the score brave souls inside.
      G   **D**   **G**
Mmm, for many a lonely day sailed across ___ the milky seas.
C*   **Em C***   **D G C***   **D**
Ne'er looked back, never feared, _____ never cried.

Chorus 1

        G
(Don't you hear my call?)

       C*
Though you're many years away.

     G   **D**
(Don't you hear me callin' you?)

     G   **B7** **Em**
Write your letters in the sand,

   G   **C***   **G**   **Am***
For ___ the day ___ I take ___ your hand

    G/B **C***   **D**   **G**
In the land that our grandchildren knew.

Interlude

E♭* E♭add♯4 E♭*	E♭6 E♭*	
Cm		A	
C	F♯m C	Am	E
B♭/F	E♭ B♭ Csus4 F	G	

Verse 2

          D   **Em**   **C***
In the year ___ of '39, came a ship ___ in from the blue.

          G   **D**
The volunteers ___ came home that day.

      Em   **Em7/D**   **C***   **Cmaj7**
And they bring good news ___ of a world ___ so newly born,

Dsus4   **D**   **G**
Though their hearts so heavily weigh.

     D   **D♯ 7**
For the earth is old and grey, little darlin', we'll away,

Em   **Am***
But my love, this cannot be.

     G   **D**   **G**
Oh, so many years have gone, though I'm older but ___ a year.

C*   **Em** **C***   **D** **G** **C***   **D**
Your mother's eyes, from your eyes, _____ cry to me.

                              G
Chorus 2   (Don't you hear my call?)
                              C*
                    Though you're many years away.
                              G   **D**
                    (Don't you hear me callin' you?)
                              G   **B7**   **Em**
                    Write your letters in the sand,
                          G   **C***   **G**   **Am***
                    For ___ the day ___ I take ___ your hand
                          G/B **C**   **D**   **G**   **D**
                    In the land that our grandchildren knew.
                                  G   **C***
                    (Don't you hear my call though you're many years away?)
                                  G   **D**
                    (Don't you hear me callin' you?)
                              G   **B7**   **Em**
                    All your letters in the sand
                          G   **C*** **G**   **Am***
                    Can-not heal ___ me like your hand.
                              Em   **D**
                    For my life still a-head, pity me.

Outro | **G**   **D** | **E**   **C** **Cmaj7** | **D** | **G**   **G5**

Guitar Chord Songbooks

Each book includes complete lyrics, chord symbols, and guitar chord diagrams.

he Beatles (A-I)

awesome reference of 100 Beatles hits, including: All My
ving • All You Need Is Love • Back in the U.S.S.R. • Can't
y Me Love • Eleanor Rigby • Get Back • A Hard Day's
ght • Hey Jude • In My Life • and more.
699558 . . . .$16.95

he Beatles (J-Y)

0 more Beatles hits, including: Lady Madonna • Let It Be
The Long and Winding Road • Love Me Do • Michelle •
volution • Sgt. Pepper's Lonely Hearts Club Band • She
ves You • Twist and Shout • When I'm Sixty-Four •
sterday • and more.
699562 . . . .$16.95

hildren's Songs

er 70 songs for kids, including: Alphabet Song • Any Dream
ll Do • The Brady Bunch • The Candy Man • Do-Re-Mi •
lelweiss • It's a Small World • Puff the Magic Dragon • The
inbow Connection • Sing • Supercalifragilisticexpialidocious
Take Me Out to the Ball Game • and more!
699539 . . . .$12.95

hristmas Carols

convenient reference of 80 Christmas carols, include: Angels
e Have Heard on High • Away in a Manger • Deck the Hall •
od King Wenceslas • The Holly and the Ivy • Jingle Bells •
y to the World • O Holy Night • Silent Night • Up on the
usetop • What Child Is This? • and more.
699536 . . . .$12.95

hristmas Songs

) Christmas favorites, including: Baby, It's Cold Outside • The
ipmunk Song • The Christmas Shoes • The Christmas Song
hestnuts Roasting on an Open Fire) • Feliz Navidad • Frosty
e Snow Man • I've Got My Love to Keep Me Warm • Rudolph
e Red-Nosed Reindeer • Silver Bells • We Need a Little
hristmas • What Are You Doing New Year's Eve? • and more.
0699537 . . . .$12.95

ric Clapton

5 of Slowhand's best, including: Badge • Bell Bottom Blues
Cocaine • I Can't Stand It • I Shot the Sheriff • Lay Down
ally • Layla • Riding with the King • Strange Brew •
nshine of Your Love • Tears in Heaven • White Room •
onderful Tonight • and more.
0699567 . . . .$14.95

ontemporary Christian

great, easy-to-use collection of just the chords and lyrics to
0 hits from today's top CCM artists. Includes: Abba (Father)
Alive • Awesome God • Don't Look at Me • El Shaddai •
ind Us Faithful • Friends • The Great Divide • He Will Carry
ou • His Strength Is Perfect • I Will Be Here • Just One •
ive Out Loud • Love Will Be Our Home • A Maze of Grace
Oh Lord, You're Beautiful • Pray • Run to You •
peechless • Testify to Love • Via Dolorosa • and more.
0699564 . . . .$14.95

Country

80 country standards, including: Abilene • Always on My Mind
• Amazed • Blue • Boot Scootin' Boogie • Breathe • Could I
Have This Dance • Crazy • Folsom Prison Blues • Friends in
Low Places • Hey, Good Lookin' • I Feel Lucky • I Hope You
Dance • Sixteen Tons • Your Cheatin' Heart • and more.
00699534 . . . .$12.95

Folksongs

80 folk favorites, including: Aura Lee • Camptown Races •
Deep River • Git Along, Little Dogies • Home on the Range •
Hush, Little Baby • Man of Constant Sorrow • Nobody Knows
the Trouble I've Seen • Scarborough Fair • When the Saints
Go Marching In • and more.
00699541 . . . .$12.95

Pop/Rock

The chords and lyrics to 80 chart hits, including: All I Wanna
Do • Closer to Free • Come Sail Away • Drops of Jupiter
(Tell Me) • Every Breath You Take • Give a Little Bit •
Heartache Tonight • I Will Remember You • Imagine • More
Than Words • Mr. Jones • Smooth • Summer of '69 •
Superman (It's Not Easy) • Time After Time • What I Like
About You • Wonderful Tonight • and more.
00699538 . . . .$14.95

Rock 'n' Roll

80 rock 'n' roll classics in one convenient collection: All
Shook Up • At the Hop • Blue Suede Shoes • Chantilly Lace •
Duke of Earl • Great Balls of Fire • It's My Party • La Bamba
• The Loco-Motion • My Boyfriend's Back • Peggy Sue • Rock
Around the Clock • Stand by Me • Surfin' U.S.A. • and more.
00699535 . . . .$12.95

HAL LEONARD GUITAR METHOD

This comprehensive method is preferred by teachers and students alike for many reasons:
- Learning sequence is carefully paced with clear instructions that make it easy to learn.
- Popular songs increase the incentive to learn to play. • Versatile enough to be used as self-instruction or with a teacher. • CD accompaniments let students have fun and sound great while practicing.

METHOD BOOKS

BOOK 1

Book 1 provides beginning instruction which covers: tuning; playing position; musical symbols; notes in first position; the C, G, G7, D, D7, A7 and Em chords; rhythms through eighth notes; strumming and picking; 100 great songs, riffs and examples. Added features are a chord chart and a selection of well-known songs, including "Ode to Joy," "Rockin' Robin," "Give My Regards to Broadway," and "Time Is on My Side."
00699010 Book $5.95
00699027 Book/CD Pack $9.95

BOOK 2

Book 2 continues the instruction started in Book 1 and covers: Am, Dm, A, E, F and B7 chords; power chords; finger-style guitar; syncopations, dotted rhythms, and triplets; Carter-style solos; bass runs; pentatonic scales; improvising; tablature; 92 great songs, riffs and examples; notes in first and second position; and more!
00699020 Book $5.95
00697313 Book/CD Pack $9.95

BOOK 3

Book 3 covers: the major, minor, pentatonic and chromatic scales; sixteenth notes; barre chords; drop D tuning; movable scales; notes in fifth position; slides, hammer-ons, pull-offs and string bends; chord construction; gear; 90 great songs, riffs and examples; and more! The CD includes 61 full-band tracks for demonstration or play-along.
00699030 Book $5.95
00697316 Book/CD Pack $9.95

COMPOSITE

Books 1, 2, and 3 bound together in an easy-to-use spiral binding.
00699040 Book $14.95
00697342 Book/CD $22.95

HAL LEONARD GUITAR METHOD DVD

For the beginning electric or acoustic guitarist
00697318 DVD $19.95

SONGBOOKS

EASY POP RHYTHMS
00697336 Book $5.95
00697309 Book/CD Pack $14.95

MORE EASY POP RHYTHMS
00697338 Book $5.95
00697322 Book/CD Pack $14.95

EVEN MORE EASY POP RHYTHMS
00697340 Book $5.95
00697323 Book/CD Pack $14.95

EASY POP MELODIES
00697281 Book $5.95
00697268 Book/CD Pack $14.95

MORE EASY POP MELODIES
00697280 Book $5.95
00697269 Book/CD Pack $14.95

EVEN MORE EASY POP MELODIES
00699154 Book $5.95
00697270 Book/CD Pack $14.95

SUPPLEMENTAL REFERENCE

ARPEGGIO FINDER
00697351 9" x 12" $5.95
00697352 6" x 9" $4.95

INCREDIBLE CHORD FINDER
00697209 9" x 12" $5.95
00697200 6" x 9" $4.95

INCREDIBLE SCALE FINDER
00695490 9" x 12" $5.95
00695568 6" x 9" $4.95

STYLISTIC METHODS

BLUES GUITAR
by Greg Koch
00697326 9" x 12" Book/CD Pack $12.95
00697344 6" x 9" Book/CD Pack $12.95

COUNTRY GUITAR
by Greg Koch
00697337 9" x 12" Book/CD Pack $12.95

JAZZ GUITAR
by Jeff Schroedl
00695359 9" x 12"Book/CD Pack $12.95

ROCK GUITAR
by Michael Mueller
00697319 9" x 12"Book/CD Pack $12.95
00697343 6" x 9" Book/CD Pack $12.95

HAL•LEONARD® CORPORATION
7777 W. BLUEMOUND RD. P.O.BOX 13819 MILWAUKEE, WI 53213